Fontainebleau

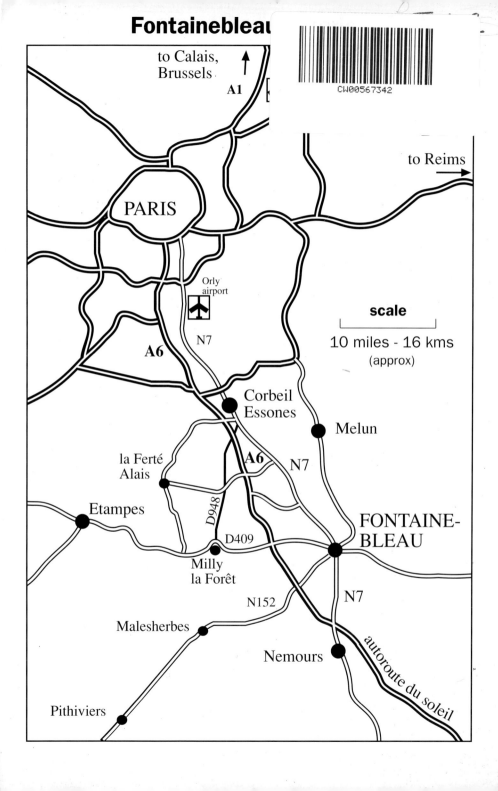

to Calais, Brussels

A1

to Reims

PARIS

Orly airport

N7

A6

scale

10 miles - 16 kms
(approx)

Corbeil Essones

Melun

la Ferté Alais

A6

N7

Etampes

D948

D409

Milly la Forêt

FONTAINE-BLEAU

N7

N152

N7

Malesherbes

Nemours

autoroute du soleil

Pithiviers

CW00567342

Fontainebleau Bouldering by
Stephen Gough

Stephen Gough © July '97

First published July '97

Produced by:
The Climbing Company Ltd
PO Box 21
Buxton
Derbyshire
SK17 9BR
Tel: (01298) 72801
Fax: (01298) 72839

Published and distributed by:
Greenshires Publishing Ltd
Telford Way
Kettering
Northants
NN16 8UN
Tel: 01536 522458
Fax: 01536 518721

Printed by:
Greenshires Print Ltd

ISBN 0-9531449-0-9

COVER PHOTOS:
Main: Gareth Parry on Uranus 7a+, Cuisinière. Paul Twomey.
Insets, top-bottom:
Le Rocher du Potala. Stéphan Denys
October morning at Cuvier. Steve Gough
Aurore Brun at Les Gorge aux Chats. Jacky Godoffe

bleau

bouldering in and around the forest of fontainebleau

CONTENTS

CONTENTS

Although I have been climbing in Fontainebleau for 20 years now, I still don't understand what drives thousands of people to repeatedly perform a strange ballet on such a collection of insignificant rocks. These people know very well how to succeed. So why do they do it? And who was the first? But even though I ask myself these questions, I don't really want an answer and I hope to be in the same state of ignorance in another twenty years.

Some claim to know more, notably about the origins of climbing in Fontainebleau. However, I know instinctively that the most respected Bleau historians, who date the start back to the time of Jacques de Lépiney, are mistaken. In the beginning there was simply a child who wanted to climb to the top of a sandstone boulder just for the sake of it. Today's "Bleausards" are simply his spiritual children. The famous alpinists of the nineteenth century were brave men in the mountains, but at Fontainebleau they were just celebrated climbers repeating what had been done before.

I think that history at Fontainebleau has come full circle, far more so than in other areas. Man came down from the trees, shed his hair, become bored with urban life and returned to the rocks...to play. In short, I believe it is the element of play, 'the game' which is the key to the bleausard style.

And yet, there is nothing to distinguish a bleausard from his fellow climbers in other continents: he shares the same culture, the same goals, the same tastes and the same appearance that go to make the ordinary climber so remarkable.

So what is it that makes Bleau so different from other climbing areas? Some would say that thanks to its marvellous rock, Bleau is one of the finest "laboratoires de mouvement" in the world. Perhaps it is simply the most beautiful climbing playground.

It is 'the game' which explains everything: moves which almost defy description; resorting to strength when a simpler method exists or, conversely, a subtle approach when strength would simplify the problem; the fascination with friction; the enigmatic low-level traverses and the (unwelcome?) remarks and advice - "oh, I do it another way!"

These characteristics could be interpreted from another viewpoint. Does the bleausard seek out complication merely for the sake of it; is he just a bull in a chinashop or is all the deft footwork a ruse to hide his fundamental lack of strength; is he meticulous to the point of insanity; is he indifferent to the thrill of the void; is he rude or a know-it-all?

No. The bleausard is simply playing and 'the game' needs rules, for ethical reasons but also, and at a more subtle level, in order to go beyond and renew them.

So welcome to the land of the "gratton" and the "aplat", clean your feet, forget the fragility of your fingertips and the incomprehensible grades and don't even think about tomorrow's aches and pains. Let your imagination fly and enjoy the elegance, fun and difficulty that Bleau has to offer. This guide will be the best of companions...

Jo Montchaussé
Barbizon,
November 19th 1996

EXPERIENCE

THE

THRILL

AT

HOME

Guarantee your copy of the climbing magazine that gives you more.

Rush me 10 issues of **ON THE EDGE** for £29.99

starting with Issue # _____*

*If left blank, subscription will start with next issue.

NAME:_____

ADDRESS:_____

_____

_____

_____

POSTCODE:_____

Payment method:

☐ Cheque enclosed   ☐ Bill my VISA/Mastercard

Offer only applies to UK Subscriptions. Overseas subscriptions, 10 issues £40.00. CHeques payable to GreenShires Publishing. Post this coupon with payment to:

GREENSHIRES PUBLISHING,
TELFORD WAY,
KETTERING,
NORTHANTS NN16 8UN

ontheedge

For many years British climbers considered Fontainebleau as little more than a stopping-off point to break the bum-numbing journey to or from the south of France, where the 'real' climbing exists. Most invariably seemed to end up at Bas Cuvier. Situated right beside one the forest's main roads, it is easy to find and has more famous problems than any other massif. The quality of the climbing and the high concentration of hard problems undoubtedly make Cuvier the mecca for hard climbing at Fontainebleau.

However, if we are to talk about quality and not just difficulty, Cuvier is only the tip of the iceberg.

Locals like to call the forest a "laboratory of movement", where a lifetime can be spent, either going to the heart of the game, in search of that elusive, fleeting moment where the impossible becomes a reality, or for those with less lofty aspirations, simply enjoying the challenge and movement that more amenable climbs have to offer.

Now that bouldering has become a fully fledged activity in its own right, Fontainebleau is an essential destination. It truly has something for everyone, from novices and children right through to those with God given talent. I hope this guide will encourage people to explore some of the lesser known areas.

Acknowledgments

Special thanks to Jo Montchauseé, Philippe le Denmat, Stéphan Denys and Marc le Menestrel. Also thanks to Benoît Faure, Jacky Godoffe, Michel Libert, Jean-Pierre Bouvier, Bernard Theret, Jean-Jacques Naël, Emmanuel Guyot and all those who gave me their 'best of' lists and the odd titbit of info. Thanks also to the good people at the library of the CAF (French Alpine Club) in Paris where I found large amounts of information. Thank you to the COSIROC, and its countless volunteers. Without their tireless work cataloguing and tracing the vast number of circuits, my job would have been much more difficult. Finally, Nigel Preston, Steve Clegg and Marile Walch for help with translations, Yvan Quehec for the Mac and Anne, without whose patience and support I would long ago have been dragged away to a secure unit for demented guidebook writers.

Stephen Gough
July '97

Salut les Francophones et bienvenue au guide de l'escalade à Fontainebleau le plus complet qu'il soit. Vous avez peut-être remarqué que le texte est écrit entièrement en anglais. Je sais, je sais, c'est un blasphème mais attendez ! Fait essentiellement de plans d'accès, de croquis detaillés et de listes, il suffit de vous souvenir de votre anglais de cinquième pour l'utiliser.

Dans les listes:

Y = yellow = jaune,	O = orange,	G = green = vert,	B = blue = bleu,
LB = light blue = bleu ciel,		R = red = rouge,	Bl = black = noir,
B/W = black and white = noir et blanc,		W = white = blanc	
b = bis, t = ter etc.			

pour les traversées   L to R = left to right = de gauche à droite
Start = départ (St. sur les croquis), end = arrivée

Par exemple:
25   16bLB 6a R to L   Le numéro 25 sur le croquis correspond au numéro 25 dans la liste; c'est le 16 bis bleu ciel, une traversée de droite à gauche côtée 6a

La carte IGN de la forêt peut s'avérer parfois bien utile, cependant, vous devriez pouvoir trouver le massif ou le bloc de votre choix uniquement avec les plans, sans vous référer au texte. Enfin, malgré le fait que personne, à ma connaissance, ne le comprenne, j'ai utilisé le système de cotation Fontainebleau partout.
Bon allez les Frenchies, à vos blocs et un de ces quatre en forêt...

Liebe Boulderfreunde! Herzlich Willkommen zum ausführlichsten Kletterführer über das französische Bouldesgebiet Fontainebleau. Natürlich haben Sie schon bemerket, daß der Text ausschließlich in englischer Sprache geschrieben ist. Ich weib, ich weib, für sämtliche Liebhaber der französischen Sprache eine Sünde, aber sicherlich ein Entgegenkommen für alle "Nichtfranzosen" mit englishen Grundkenntwissen. Die karte IGN des Waldes kann manchmal sehr nützlich sein. Abgesehen davon müßten Sie aber auch, ohne sich auf den Text zu beziehen, in der Lage sein den gewünschten Felsen ausfindig zu machen. Für alle Boulderprobleme habe ich die Bewertungsskala von Fontainebleau benutzt.
Viel Spaß und bis bald im Wald... von Fontainebleau.

In den Listen:
Y = gelb,   O = orange,   G = grün,   B = blau,   LB = hellblau,   R = rot,
Bl = schwarz,   W = weis,   B/W = schwarz und weis

für Quergänge
L to R = links nach rechts
Start = Start (St. in den shizzen)
End = Ende

Zum ßeispiel:
25 16bLB 6a R nach L   Die Nummer 25 in der Skizze entspricht der Nummer 25 in der Liste das ist der 16 bis hellblau, ein Quergang von rechts nach links Grad 6a.

The unique character of the Fontainebleau style and the extreme difficulty of the hardest problems is the fruit of a long history, which started at the beginning of the century. The great leaps forward invariably took place at Cuvier or Cuvier Rempart. This was initially because it was simply one of the most easily accessible massifs.

Here are a few dates:

1908 At Cuvier Rempart the hideous crack between Duroxmanie and Le Carré d'As is climbed (in nailed boots!) by Jacques Wehrlin, one of a group of French Alpine Club members who first began to use the forest as an alpine training ground.

1913 L'Arête de Larchant at La Dame Jouanne is soloed by Jacques de Lepiney who also introduces the use of rope-soled espadrilles.

1914 La Fissure de la Prestat at Cuvier is climbed by the same.

1934 La Fissure des Alpinistes at Apremont is climbed by Pierre Allain. The first grade five and still no pushover, especially if you try and off-width it!

1935 Piere Allain tests the first prototypes of his famous 'PAs' which I assume he was wearing for his very tricky "Angle Allain" at Cuvier Rempart, then graded six and since downgraded to 5+.

1938 Hugh Paillon climbs la Paillon Directe at Cuvier, which is today the last problem of the famous blue circuit. The finishing holds are 'sculpted', a trend which is set to increase...

1945 The first guide is published by Maurice Martin. Names and approximate (aren't they always!) grades are painted on the boulders.

1946 The first official 6a in the forest, La Marie Rose at Cuvier, is climbed by René Ferlet. Despite sticky rubber the grade remains the same today.

1947 The forest's first circuit, the red at Cuvier Rempart, is traced by Fred Bernick.

1948 Pierre Allain finally markets his PAs.

1950 Paul Jouy climbs la Stalingrade (6b) and La Carré d'As (6c) at Cuvier. Still bold today, repeats are not numerous. Cuvier is already well established as the spiritual home of Fontainebleau bouldering.

1952 Michel Dufranc climbs le Quatrième Angle at Cuvier, still graded 6c.

1953 Robert Paragot manages Le Joker at Cuvier, then graded 6f, before the arrival of the seventh degree. Today it's 7a! All these climbers shared their passion for Bleau with their alpine and himalayan exploits. For the majority Bleau is still a training ground for the mountains.

1956 The first hard circuit is traced, la 'Fraise Ecrasée' at Apremont. Giving climbing in the fourth and fifth grade, today it is one of the quietest circuits in the forest.

1960 Well ahead of its time, Abbatoir, the first uncontested 7a is climbed by Michel Libert. It still inspires countless climbers. Like his friend Robert Paragot, Michel can still be seen climbing at Cuvier. Respect! In this period the white circuit, which will be added to by future generations, begins to take shape. Michel Libert climbs it in big boots!

1964 The epic 'Salmon' circuit is traced at Apremont by Jacques Reppelin and Pierre Porta. Its 74 problems have been done in 45 minutes.

1967 The COSIROC has taken shape and begins to co-ordinate, in liaison with the ONF (National Forestry Office) the growing number of circuits. Taking over from Lucien Deschamps and Pierre Bontemps in 1975, Oleg Sokolsky has been one of the main figures involved, still tirelessly co-ordinating this colossal task.

1968 Attention begins to shift from Cuvier with the tracing of two classic white circuits at Cuisinière and 95.2 by Patrick Cordier.

1972 Two classic black circuits combining high technical difficulty with the need for a cool head. Buthiers (piscine) by Alain Michaud and les Gros Sablons by Jacques Olivet.

1977 Jérome Jean-Charles climbs Carnage, the first 7b. One of many problems where chipping was used to overcome a seemingly impossible problem. Still perhaps the most covetted problem of its grade in the forest. Along with Thierry Bienvenu (la Défroquée one handed (do it with 2 already!) and the Cuvier red in 18 minutes!!!) he strived to maintain the element of play in bouldering, trying to find bizarre and delicate movements where climbing a boulder is "a succession of resting positions."

1978 Le Toit du Cul de Chien is climbed by Eddy Bouchet and Jo Montchaussé. Not a step forward in terms of difficulty but one of the forest's great problems.

By the early '80s a new generation is beginning to come forward; Alain Ghersen, Antoine and Marc le Menestrel, Jacky Godoffe and Jo Montchaussé (the latter three still as keen as ever) to name but a few.

1980 A two year war breaks out between those who prefer a 'back to nature' approach ie. no circuits, and proponents of the COSIROC approach. Systematic tracing, scrubbing out and retracing of circuits.

1982 Sticky rubber appears!

1983 Pierre Richard climbs la Bérézina at Cuvier, the first 7c, completing the most famous trio of hard problems in the forest. Jerry Moffatt blitzes Cuvier on his first visit, leaving the locals speechless. Le Surplomb de la Mée is climbed by Messrs. Godoffe and Ghersen and given a tentative 7c+ grade. After a broken hold Marc le Menestrel was the only one able to repeat it until very recently. Now graded 8a+ and one of the lines of the forest.

1984 Jacky Godoffe climbs C'Etait Demain at Cuvier Rempart, the first uncontested 8a. Like le Surplomb de la Mée, a good example of where precision, power and technique combine to make a very hard climb. Jean-Michel Gosselin climbs la Super Prestat (7b+) at Cuvier, a landmark slab climb.

1986 More grade eights are proposed. Ghersen climbs Ange Naïf at 95.2 (since downgraded to 7c+), Godoffe climbs la Balance (easier methods now exist) at Cuvier and together they climb Partenaire Particulier (unrepeated since) at l'Elephant.

1987 Alain Ghersen succeeds in climbing all problems graded 7a and above.

1988 Rempart's fine trio of Big Boss, Fourmis Rouges and Tristesse, first climbed by

Jacky Godoffe, becomes a quartet with Olivier Carrière's ascent of Big Golden. Olivier goes on to add the similarly necky T. Rex nearby.

1989 With natural unclimbed lines becoming scarce, eliminates and traverses begin to grow in popularity. Philippe le Denmat climbs Golden Feet at Cuvier, a major step forward in slab climbing difficulty. Remarkable not for the beauty or purety of the line but for the fact that there are no holds! Jacky Godoffe climbs the never-ending Mouvement Perpetuel 8b at Cuvier. This awesome traverse waits four years for a repeat at the hands of the mighty Benoît Faure who becomes one of the keenest devotees of the horizontal game (Les Yeux..., Voltane).

1991 Young and gifted David Rastouil just pips Jacky Godoffe to the post on the magnificent Rubis sur l'Ongle (or was it the ultra-discreet Antoine le Menestrel?) Just before leaving the area he manages Carnage, la Bérézina, la Balance, Infidèle, Hypothèse, Michel Ange, Big Boss, Fourmis Rouges, Tristesse and Big Golden all first try in the same session.

1993 The first straight up 8bs are climbed and await confirmation. Philippe le Denmat confirms his extraordinarily high pain tolerance and predeliction for steep walls and slabs (L'Ange Gardien, Plein Vol, Duel etc) with Enigma at Isatis while Jacky Godoffe climbs Fatman at Cuvier Rempart.

1997 In February Marc le Menestrel succeeds on his long-standing project at Apremont. L'Alchimiste is only the forest's third proposed straight-up 8b.

And the future?

The scene is healthy, with many incredibly keen individuals opening up new areas and unearthing new problems. Tensions surrounding chipping and the use of sica have calmed but not entirely disappeared. The messy reinforcement with sica of a famous hold at Cuvier in early '97 shows that the purists do not have it all their own way. The future of the circuit is unclear; some would like to see a more limited role for the COSIROC. One trend is the searching out of isolated problems. The dream is to stumble across the ultimate boulder during your rest day stroll in the woods...

A s a general rule there are between seven and eight levels of difficulty. This can vary quite wildly within a given circuit, especially if the 'bis' problems are included.

Approx. UK comparisons

WHITE	Easy
YELLOW	Up to 4b
ORANGE	Up to 4c
BLUE	4c to 5c
(LIGHT BLUE)	5a to 6b
RED	5a to 6b
BLACK	5b to 6c/7a
WHITE	5c to 6c/7a

A black can be harder than a white, eg, Cuisinière.

The more traditional circuits have been marked with a view to doing the entire circuit in one go, sometimes without touching the ground. These circuits have many more arrowed boulders than there are numbered problems. This is a rather old fashioned approach but still popular with some.

Although most boulderers pick and choose boulders more or less at random, the circuit, if comfortably within your limit, can be either an excellent way to warm up, or a good way to discover a new massif.

The COSIROC (Committee for the defence of rocks and climbing sites) is a voluntary organisation formed in the '60s to coordinate the tracing of circuits in the forest. It's an umbrella group comprising numerous sports associations in the region. The COSIROC liaises with the ONF (Forestry Commission), which gives the go ahead (or not) to new circuits. Today there are around 200 in existence. Things have moved on a little since the old days, when some circuits looked as if they'd been painted with a big dog's nose. Now the trend is towards small, discreet arrows and numbers.

Although the circuits have played a very important role in the development of climbing at all levels in the forest, many are beginning to question the need to create new ones and of constantly modifying those already in existence.

IMPORTANT NOTE: the COSIROC periodically reviews the state of the circuits. It's rare for a circuit to be retraced without modifications and it doesn't take many number changes to alter the entire circuit. This is a constant problem for a Fontainebleau guidebook writer and anyone who would like the circuits to provide a permanent reference point for other problems. So beware. At Rocher Canon for example, the red circuit has been extensively altered and a new B/W circuit created. Nobody asked for this and I have not bothered incorporating the new numbers in the lists. Isatis is also due for a major overhaul. So if a number in the list doesn't correspond to the boulder in front of you it's probably because the COSIROC got there between this guide going to print and your visit.

Fontainebleau grades have been used throughout this guide. I've never been to Hueco and using UK grades would have meant doing every problem in the guide, a somewhat unrealistic prospect.

So how do they work?

Fontainebleau grades can only be compared to French cliff grades in the sense that they try to take all aspects of the climb into account. Is the difficulty sustained or is there only one hard move? Is the landing good or will you break every bone in your body? etc etc. For the better British climbers frustration can creep in when they arrive thinking they'll be able to waltz up the 7as. Frustration approaches humiliation when the 5+s start posing problems (mumblings of "shouldn't be difficult, I did a Font 7b in the Peak only last week...").

There are several possible explanations for this difficulty. The boulderer is perhaps confusing bouldering and cliff grades (a Font 7a is perhaps a7c/8a crux on a crag) or perhaps previous coverage of Fontainebleau has given misleading comparisons with UK technical grades. Let's not forget that Font 5+ is hard! You can redpoint 7c and still fail on one. And of course, Peak Font 7b is not Font 7b.

The infinite variety of moves and technical puzzles and the varying morphology of those who have climbed and graded them means that difficulty is specific to each problem. When you combine this with the difference that good conditions can make and the importance of finding the knack (even on relatively 'easy' problems) it becomes clear that no system can hope to reflect all these ingredients accurately.

So, the Fontainebleau grading system is something of a mystery, an imperfect solution that provides a guide and no more. I'm told a fuller understanding comes with (years of) experience and 'feeling'. Don't get frustrated!

For traverses the system is slightly different. As a very rough guide, if you can do a straight up 5 you should in theory be able to manage a 6a traverse. A straight up 7a, a 7c traverse and so on. Stamina withstanding of course. Here is a proposal for a slightly revised grading comparison, particularly in the Font 4 to 6c bracket, the level at which the vast majority operate.

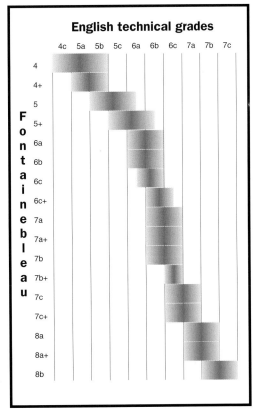

English technical grades

For most massifs you shouldn't need the text to get to the problems. The maps should be self explanatory. However it's worth having the IGN map of the forest (available in most local newsagents and petrol stations) to fill in any gaps and go exploring in bad weather or rest days.

Area access maps

More or less to scale. On these I've marked the start of any circuits which start outside the boulder plans and, with a number, the location of any off-the-beaten-track but worthwhile problems which are then listed in the area introduction. The location of the boulder plans is also marked.

Boulder plans

These are not to scale and should be used with a dose of common sense in which case you'll find your chosen circuit or problem with little difficulty. Black dots on the boulder plans are straight up problems. Black triangles are traverses. Both are in the lists. On some of the 'busier' plans I've left out the occasional number for clarity. Small circles are problems not in the list. Sometimes I've marked the initial of the colour next to the circle.

Lists

As an example...

34 4R 5+	Number 34 on the plan is the 4 red, graded 5+
35 6bLB 5 L to R	Number 35 on the plan is the 6 bis (a bis is a variant) light blue, a left-right traverse graded 5
36 6c	An unmarked problem graded 6c

Sometimes grades and/or circuit numbers were not available in which case only the colour is marked on the list, which should be enough to give you a rough idea of the difficulty.

I've tried to include the best of the (mostly harder) unmarked problems but some will have slipped through the net. As the number of games and variants are only limited by your imagination a complete guide is an impossibility. In any case there's enough to keep you busy for years!

Throughout the guide the following abbreviations have been used:

Y = yellow   O = orange B = blue   R = red
Bl = black   LB = light blue   B/W = black and white
St. = start   R to L = right to left traverse.

WHEN TO COME

You've been trying to hang that sloper for what seems like an eternity. And one day you will. Not because you're stronger or better but because the magical ingredients have all combined to make conditions perfect. Or as the locals say, "ça colle!" literally, "it sticks." For the harder problems the best time to come is between November and February. It must be cold between 0 (if you're as hard as nails) and 8°C. Low humidity and a stiff breeze help enormously and can make conditions good in warmer weather, say in October or March. However it's impossible to generalise. Best to try and get a long-range weather forecast before coming out. For climbers with more modest aspirations fun is available all year round although even the 'easy' problems can become considerably harder in the summer heat.

WHERE TO STAY

Camping

The best option is almost cetainly La Musardière, near Milly. Ideal for Les Trois Pignons and centrally located for all the areas in this guide. Plenty of shade. Open from February 15th to December 15th. Per night: 25F per person, 14F per car, 12F per tent.

The free campsite near Bas Cuvier is popular with hitchhikers (ease of access), cheapskates and students. It's a little over 1km NW of Cuvier, opposite the turning for Barbizon. No facilities and you may return to find all your gear has been stolen.

Just outside (north) of Bourron-Marlotte, about 16kms south of Fontainebleau on the N7, is another free campsite with water. Further from the main areas but a good alternative to Cuvier when it's busy and if you have transport.

At Samoreau, just east of Fontainebleau there's a municipal campsite open from March 15th to October 31st.

Hotels

Various cheapish hotels in Fontainebleau where you may be able to negotiate a third person sleeping on the floor in a double room. For details ring the Fontainebleau tourist office 01 60 74 99 99.

Gites

As one well chuffed Sheffield visitor exclaimed, "It's better than living at home!" Most of the villages in and around the forest have gites, some of which are more like palaces. If you're coming with a crowd in winter it's probably the best bet, budget permitting. Phone, fax or write Le Comité Régional du Tourisme, 26 Avenue de l'Opéra, 75001 PARIS, telephone 01 42 60 28 62, fax 01 42 60 20 23.

Bed 'n' Breakfast

Excellent, laid back sevice in a self contained flat in Fontainebleau. Contact Barbara le Van Huy on 01 64 22 29 30.

For other enquiries you can ring the regional tourist office (Seine et Marne) on 01 64 10 10 64.

WHERE TO SHOP
For food
There's a huge shopping centre at Villiers-en-Bière, 4kms north of Chailly-en-Bière (just north of Barbizon) on the N7. M&S for baked beans, the rest at Carrefour. Open till 10 in the week, 9 on Saturdays. Closed on Sunday.
On the D948 1km south of Milly-la-Forêt, there's an Intermarché, open from 9 to 7.20 (closed 12.20 to 3), Monday to Saturday and 9 to 12.20 on Sunday morning. Milly also has a couple of corner shops just off the market square (west) that stay open late.
For those into turnips, Arbonne has several outlets for this underrated vegetable.
For climbing gear
Decathlon at Villiers-en-Bière.
At weekends Sebastien Wilmot at the Trois Pignons centre carpark does a good resoling service.

WHERE TO EAT AND DRINK
The forest has a distinct lack of places to unwind after a day out, especially if you want to meet other climbers. A few places however give simple food and drink within staggering distance of the boulders: the bar in Barbizon, the Chalet Jobert at La Dame Jouanne, the Auberge Canard at Buthiers and La Chaumière (particularly good) at Beauvais, where it's well worth reserving a table outside if you're there in summer (tel: 01 64 98 04 71).

WHERE TO GO WHEN IT RAINS
You can climb at Calvaire in just about all weathers. Otherwise...
Walls
Mur-Mur Claims to be the biggest climbing centre in Europe. Open seven days a week. Includes sauna, weights room and bar. 55 rue Cartier Bresson, NE Paris, just outside le boulevard péripherique (Porte de la Villette).
Le Centre Européen de l'Escalade In the southern outskirts of Paris at Thiais, next to the N7 and near to the Belle Epine shopping centre, opposite Decathlon.
There are also plans for a wall in Larchant, near to l'Eléphant and la Dame Jouanne.
WHERE TO GO WHEN IT'S TOO HOT
There's an outdoor swimming pool next to the football pitch by the D16 as you leave Milly for the Trois Pignons. Open 10 to 7, every day through July and August. There's also an indoor pool here, open all year round.
Buthiers also has a superb outdoor pool right next to the boulders. Open from 10 to 7.15 from the end of May to the beginning of September.
Otherwise wine, beer and other drinks are widely available here and the forest is not short of trees to sit under...

CHILDREN
Apremont
Beauvais
Roche aux Sabots
Eléphant

FIRST STEPS
Beauvais
Rocher St Germain
Le Rocher de la Reine
Diplodocus
Mont Ussy
Les Rochers des Potets
Eléphant

SOMETHING FOR EVERYONE
Beauvais
Apremont
Isatis/Hautes Plaines
Eléphant

RAINY DAY CLIMBING
Calvaire

PEACE AND QUIET
La Padole
Le Restant du Long Rocher
Videlles/Les Roches
Les Béorlots

TRAINING FOR EVEREST
Cuisinière (Orange mountain circuit)
Les Gros Sablons (Orange no.1)
La Dame Jouanne (Mauve or Yellow)

SUMMER SHADE
Anywhere really, except most of les Trois
Pignons and les Gorges d'Apremont

QUICK DRYING & WINTER WARMTH
Les Gorges d'Apremont
95.2
Cul de Chien
91.1
Rocher Fin
JA Martin

ARMBLASTERS
Roche aux Sabots
Eléphant

FINGER WRECKERS
Cuisinière
95.2
Le Rocher du Potala
Rocher Fin

HORIZONTAL FUN
Beauvais
La Canche aux Merciers

ADRENALIN RUSH GUARANTEED
La Padôle
Rocher Gréau
Puiselet
La Dame Jouanne
Buthiers

"It's a bit more technical than I expected."
Malcolm Smith, after his first day at Bleau.

Don't forget... your feet! Or in other words, technique. Even our best exports are accused of lacking it. Few good bleausards have the stick-man physique of a sport climber. Broad shoulders and bumpy arms perhaps, but in place of the two sticks that hang uselessly from the sport climbers' waist, you're more likely to find a pair of pins that Big Mig would be proud of and a bum that actually fills the wearer's tights!

The true bleausard often uses his feet with such guile that the visitor may almost consider it as cheating. Crafty (or at least good) footwork, if not absolutely essential for the awesomely strong, certainly brings the grades tumbling for lesser mortals on many problems. So forget plyometrics and get practising those heel and toe hooks. El Poussah (Isatis) or le Cul de Chien may be your reward. See "no hands" list.

CHALK v RESIN

This one will run and run. Still a very touchy subject with some although more and more use chalk as well as resin. It's still not uncommon to get your ear bent by some outraged traditionalist who will insist that chalk is ugly and has a long term negative effect on the rock.

Resin is normally used on fingers or footholds to increase sticking power.. It does not have a benign effect on the rock and like chalk, it too can be an eyesore. A good mat, clean holds and clean rubber will reduce the need for it. It is not tolerated in the UK so why use it here? Moderation is the best policy and in really good conditions you should feel very little need, if any, for either resin or chalk.

**Stéphane Guyon on Le Pilier Droyer
6c+, Eléphant.** Alain Hoffman

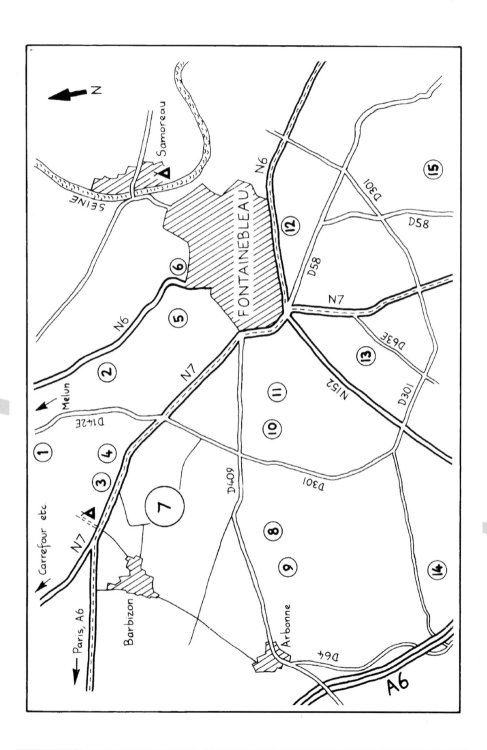

NORTH

1 Rocher Canon
2 Rocher St Germain
3 Bas Cuvier
4 Cuvier Rempart
5 Mont Ussy
6 Calvaire
7 Apremont

CENTRE

8 Franchard Cuisinière
9 Franchard Isatis, Sablons,
Hautes Plaines
10 Les Gorges du Houx
11 Mont Aigu
12 Rocher d'Avon

SOUTH

13 Rocher des Demoiselles
14 Les Béorlots
15 Restant du Long Rocher

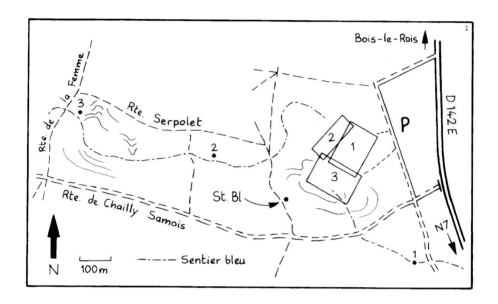

Plan 2

DIRECTIONS

On the N7, roughly midway between Cuvier and Fontainebleau there is a big set of traffic lights. Take the D142E north-eastwards, direction Melun. The road descends, bearing left. Soon after it trends gently right. Just after this, about 3.5 kms after the lights, take an easy to miss left turn which leads into the woods, then left again to the parking.

From the other direction, the turn for the parking is just under 2 kms south of the crossroads formed by the D142E and the D115.

Walk past the boulders nearest the parking, passing the start of a good children's circuit, and problem 1, plan 1 is just after.

CHARACTER

A superb massif, one of the best in the forest. It gets enough shade to be worth a visit during the summer but also dries fairly quickly after rain.

CLIMBING

White (children's 22 problems)
Yellow PD (40 problems)
Orange AD+ (37 problems)
Blue D (42 problems)
Light Blue TD- (40 problems)
Red ED- Has been needlesly retraced since time of writing
Black ED and B/W ED+

There's a wealth of brilliant climbing here, landings are generally good and the climbing is varied; technicians and thugs alike will find something to keep them happy.

For the start of the black circuit follow the Route de Laisser Courre west for about 400m. Turn R at an obvious crossroads and the start is just off to the R of the path after about 150m.

There are a few off the beaten track traverses that are worth the walk. They're marked on the map...

1 Miracle 7a R to L. Finish up the prow. Located on the sentier bleu.

2 L'Académicienne 6c L to R. This long vertical wall is just below (north) of the sentier bleu. Look hard!

3 Trois Graines d'Eternité 7b+ R to L. Use the big jug as a hold, an unusual no hands rest, or miss it out altogether and up the grade. Situated just off the sentier bleu (north), shortly before it crosses the Route de la Femme.

1	**1B 4-**
2	2B 3-
3	3B 4
4	**R 5+**
5	START Blue
6	7c+ L to R
7	R 5
8	R 6b
9	**R Puzzle 5+**
10	**R Magifix 6a/b**
11	4B 4-
12	Old 27R 5
13	6c+ L to R
14	**22B 4-**
15	5B 3-
16	**6B 3+**
17	7B 4+
18	**8B 5-**
19	24LB 4+
20	9B 5-
21	**R 5+ R to L**
22	23LB 4
23	19O 3-
24	22LB 4-
25	13B 4
26	14B 3+
27	**25LB Le Surplomb du Bengale 5**
28	**30R Nuage Blanc 6b**
29	15B 4-
30	16B 4+
31	17B 4+
32	18B 5-
33	19B 4
34	20B 4+
35	21B 4+
36	**Manus Dei 8a L to R Exit R of 25**
37	O
38	12B 4-
39	**21LB La Bendix 5**
40	10B 4+
41	11B 4
42	20LB La Contralto 5
43	19LB 4-
44	R 6a L to R
45	**18LB La Soprano 5-**
46	**15LB L'Emmental 5**
47	**R Bateau-pilote 6a+**
48	24O
49	17LBb 5+
50	17LB Le Cruciverbiste 5
51	R 5+
52	**16LB Le Cheval d'Arçon 5**
53	**23O 3+**
54	**R Le Styrax 6a**
55	**6c**
56	**R 5**
57	**30LB 4**
58	31LB Le Prétoire 4+
59	29LB 4-
60	28LB 5-
61	27LB 4
62	R 5+
63	**40Y**
64	**26LB 5-**
65	R 5+
66	32B
67	**R Saillie d'Esprit 6c**

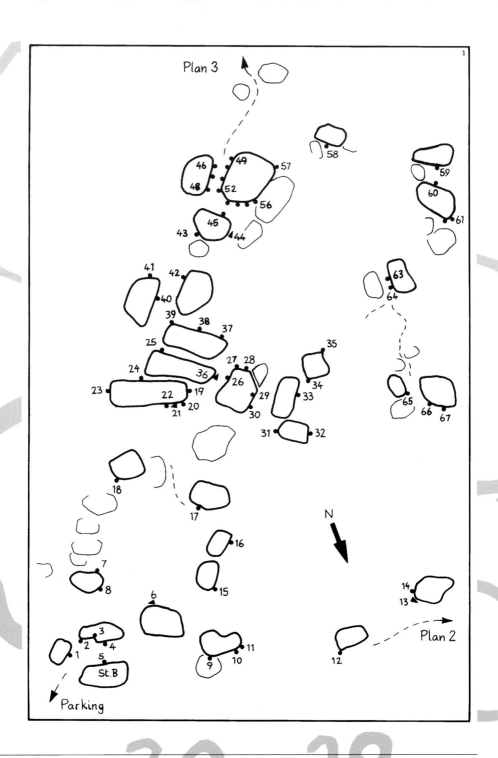

1 R 6a R to L
2 R 5+
3 R 5+
4 4+
5 R 5+
6 Cocaline 7c R to L Finish up 3
7 R 5+
8 Crescendo R to L 7b+ for an exit up 9, 7c+ for 10.
9 bR
10 R 6a
11 28B 4
12 R 6a
13 23B 3+
14 R 5
15 24B 3+
16 27B 3
17 26B 4-
18 25B 3
19 31B 4-
20 30B 5-
21 La Levitation 7a L to R to exit up crack.
Le Vagabond des Limbes 7b goes back L along lip to finish up R. Legende 8a continues L to start of Levitation.
22 R 5+
23 Sledgehammer 6c R to L
24 R 5
25 35B 4+
26 36B 4
27 38B 4
28 37B 4
29 39B 4+
30 40B 4-   END Blue
31 R Boomerang 5+

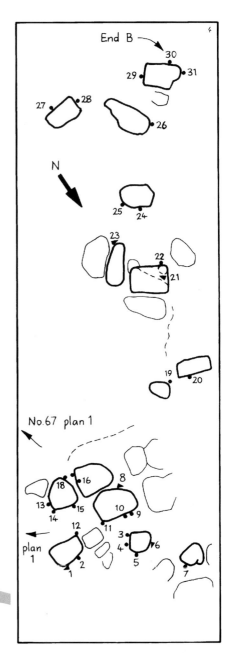

METOLIUS

01457 8770 81

Jason Karn product testing at
Smith Rock, Oregon

1 R Le Whist 6a
2 R Le Bossu 6b
3 33LB La Voie de l'Obèse 4
4 34LB 4+
5 O R to L
6 13LB La Queue du Dromadaire 4
   13b 4+
7 12LB Le Beaufort 4
8 16O
9 14LB L'Imprévue 4+
10 35LB 4
11 13O R to L
12 8LB Le Sphinx 4
13 9LB Le Golgotha 4
14 R 6a R to L
15 36LB Le Serpent 4+
16 R 6a
17 37LB Le French Cancan 4
18 Deliverance 7a Direct on 19
19 R 6c Up and L
20 40LB Le Cervin 5-   END Light Blue
21 39LB 5
22 R Le Jeu de Go 5+
23 38LB 5-
24 R 5-
25 R 5
26 R Adrénaline 5+
27 R Coup de Poker 5-
28 19Bl
29 22Bl
30 23Bl
31 R Presse-citron 5+
32 R Jets Interdits 6a
33 R 5-
34 26Bl
35 34O
36 R L'Ancien 5+
37 Rb Dure Limite 6b
38 Le Bloc de la Mare
   R 6a+ and a **7b/c** to its R. Another starts up the R and crosses the 7b/c before exiting, 7b+. Sadly, the top of this boulder is a bit of an eyesore since a local environmentalist attemted to cement up the holds in protest at the draining of the slime-filled pool which occasionally forms at its foot.

39 7LB 4
40 36.15 Power 7c+ Strictly for brutes. An easier variant reaches out L to the arete, then back R.
41 6LB L'Attrape Mouche 5
42 5LB 4+
43 R 5
44 4LB 6a
45 3LB 4+
46 R 5/6b
47 2LB 4+
48 R 5-
49 Le Chaînon Manquant 7c+/8a? This bizarre problem zig-zags its way up the wall below the leaning tree using flatties on R before leaping L. Nasty landing.
50 R Force G 6a
51 La Valse aux Adieux 8b Desperate L to R traverse.
52 1LB 5-   START Light Blue
53 O   START Orange
54 R 6b
55 R 5+ Thin crack
56 R 5+ The fine, bold arete
57 Caterpillare 7a+
58 Chasseur de Prises 7a+. A well hidden gem and a must at the grade. A cheating stone barely makes it easier.

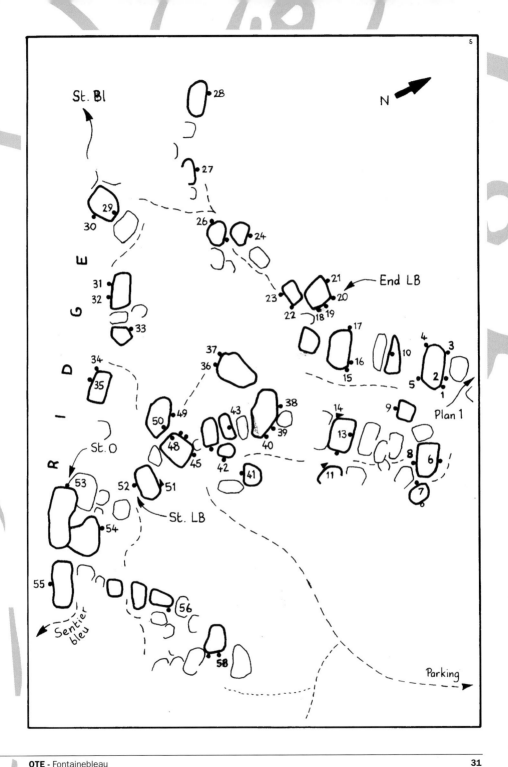

DIRECTIONS

Follow the N6 north out of Fontainebleau. About 3 kms out of the town and 750m after a L turn for the racetrack (Hippodrome de la Salle) park at a large car park on the left (be careful turning onto it). The Route de Luxembourg cuts into the forest from here. See map for access to circuits.

The hard problems can be reached from the above car park. Alternatively, park at the west end of the massif at the Carrefour de Belle Croix, on the D142E (as for Rocher Canon), 1.3 kms from the N7. Follow the Route de Luxembourg eastwards into the forest. The path for problems 1 and 2 is easy to miss. It wriggles off L shortly after a prominent flat stone on the R side of the path. Trend L at first, then a R turn takes you to the foot of "Les Yeux…" Behind this there's a sentier bleu. Follow this R a short way and you'll see Mégalithe off to the R. You can follow the sentier bleu for the other problems or stick to the Route de Luxembourg and turn L at the clearing.

CHARACTER

Quiet and shady. Good in summer but slow to dry in winter.

CLIMBING

White (children's 51 problems)
Yellow PD+ (50 problems)
Orange
Blue D+ (39 problems)

Good varied climbing in a quiet setting. The blue includes some fine and tricky problems while the rest provides a good outing for lower level climbers.

Further west there hide several modern classics that the locals would like to keep to themselves :

1 Les Yeux plus gros que le Ventre 7c+ R to L Start below the prominent jug. Futuristic straight ups waiting to be done.

2 Mégalithe 8a? Superb, dynamic climbing

3 Double Croche 7b+ L to R. And in the obvious long narrow corridor…

4 Danse de Printemps 7b+/8a R to L from R arete to exit either on slopes just L of corridor or, much harder, round the L arete.

5 Psychose 7c+ low, (8a high?)

6 7b+ R to L Situated in another corridor on the sentier bleu.

7 La Cité Perdue 7c+ (aka la Vie devant soi) R to L

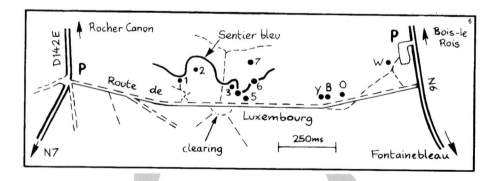

DIRECTIONS

The car park is on the N7, about 5 kms NW of Fontainebleau. Approaching from the north, it's the first car park as you come into the forest, about 1.25 kms after the petrol station (on the L) and the R turn for Barbizon. From Fontainebleau, it's after the big set of lights on the junction with the D301 and the D142E. The first problems lie a few metres from the car park.

CHARACTER

The busiest massif in the forest. For an area with so much shade it dries remarkably quickly so it's worth visiting all year round, although in summer you'll struggle (even more) on the harder problems. If you don't mind crowds, polished holds and at times a rather intense atmosphere you'll love it.

CLIMBING

Orange AD- (50 probs) A classic and perhaps the hardest orange in the forest. Very polished.

Blue D- No 1 (26 probs) Quiet. Nos. 9, 10 and 22 are worth hunting out.

Blue TD- No 7 (48 probs) Essential bleausard apprenticeship. Varied and technical.

Blue TD No 4 (50 probs) Quiet. Inconsistent in terms of difficulty (3 to 6a), it nevertheless has some fine problems

Red TD+ (42 probs) Another must do circuit with no dull moments.

Black ED- (30 probs) Varied, spread out and hard. Many classic problems.

White ED+ (17 probs) This takes you to the heart of the Fontainebleau game and has enough to keep most of us busy for years.

Plus millions of unmarked problems. Love it or hate it, Bas Cuvier is the mecca for hard climbing at Fontainebleau. But it also reflects perfectly the history of bouldering in the forest, with a wide degree of difficulty available. Purists will scowl at the numerous chipped holds but they form an important part in the development of climbing here. All the circuits (except the blues 1 and 4) are considered essential rites of passage for those who take their bouldering seriously. Landings are generally good. Don't be intimidated by the locals; they're (normally) only too happy to give advice to floundering visitors.

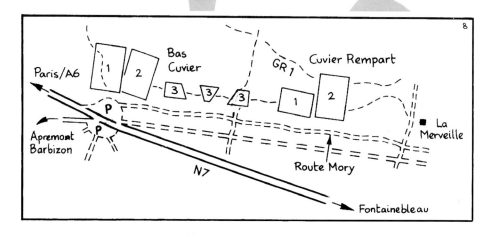

The first two boulders mark the start of four classic circuits: blue, red, black and white.

1   60 2
2   1B Le Sans les Mains 5   START Blue
3   La Croix de Fer 7b
4   1Bl 6a   START Black
5   1R 5+   START Red
6   2B 4+
7   1W La Lili 6c   START White
8   bB 4+
9   70 3+
10   2R 5+
11   3B 5-
12   3R 5+
13   90 3
14   170 2+
15   Doigté 6b R to L
16   16 0 3-
17   16tB 4+
18   3bB 4+
19   150 2+
20   16bB 4+ The fine artete to the left is **Le Poinçonneur des Lilas 7a/b**
21   La Spoutnik 6b+
22   7Bl Scampi Fritté 6c
23   11R 5+
24   16B 5
25   10R La Bijou 5
     Just L is the **15B 4+**
26   7B Le Coq Droite 4+
27   6B Le coq 4+
28   4Bl 5
29   5B 4-
30   5R La Genouillère 5+ So called because of the temptation to use a knee on the last move.
31   120 2
32   4B 5+ Just R **Le Mur du Feu 7a+**
     Just L L'Ovomaltine 6b+
33   100 3
34   110 2
35   2W L'Emporte Pièce 6a
36   4R Le Trou du Simon 6a
37   Bb 4
38   2bW L'Aérodynamite 7b+ No cheating stone if you want a 7b+ tick

39   3B 4+
40   2Bl 5+
41   Platinum 7a
42   2bB 5
43   La Tonsure 7a Up the slope is the superb **Fluide Magnetique 7b**
44   4B 4
45   5B 4+
46   270 3-
47   6B 3
48   7B 4
49   300 2+
50   12B La Dalle du Réveil-matin 4+
51   13B 5
52   Vadou-Système 6c, moves out R to the slopes on the arete. Just to the L is Mal en Tendu 6b+.
53   6c+/7a L to R
54   Sanguine 6b
55   Béatrice 6b
56   Le Coin Arrière 6a
57   Raideur Digeste 7c+
58   6c L to R
59   Le Sang Lisse 6b L to R and up
60   310 2-
61   Voyage à l'Envers 5+ L to R, exit at jug; 6a+ with return trip.

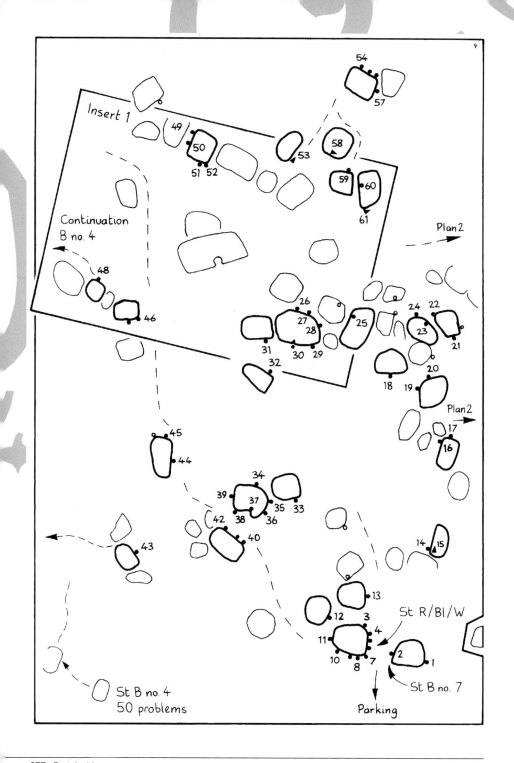

1 3W Le Dernier Jeu 6a
2 3bW La Ravensbruck 6b
3 8B La Poule 4-
4 6R La Gugusse 5+
5 250 Le Mur aux Fênes 3-
6 5Bl La Salade 6a
7 6b Mantel onto the obvious flake. Also here, Photo Sensible 7c R to L from flake to finish up no 6.
8 8R La vire Authenac 5
9 7R Les Frites 5+
10 Le Mouvement Perpétuel 8b An awesome R to L traverse, finishing up 16, with a loop thrown in for good measure. After downclimbing crux of 15, traverse low back R into 14, doing its crux to regain the traverse. Down 15 again, L and up 16 to finish. Done in 1989 and only one repeat to date.
11 11B 4+
12 Pendule de Foucault 8a As for 10 but avoids a hard move at the start.
13 5W La Boucherie 7a
14 L'Araignée 7a Take a deep breath, push off and believe! Finish up 15.
15 4W Charcuterie 6c+/7a Harder if done static to the undercuts; otherwise lunge for the hold just above.
16 4bW L'Angle Incarné 7b
17 9B 4+
18 Antithèse 7c+ Same starting hold as 19 but moves up and R
19 L'Hypothèse 7c Central 'line' from painful starting crimp
20 L'Infidèle 7c+
21 280 3-
22 10B 4+
23 Pince-mi, Pince-moi 7b+ Very powerful from back of roof, as is...
24 Vert Clair 7b+ Start low by black dot on25 then up and long span out to lip.
25 6Bl Le Biceps Mou 7a+ Standing start by black dot and thug out R.
26 Holey-Moley 7a Out and up via slopes.

There are various desperate traverses on this boulder...
Obsession 7c+ Traverses R from L of 23 to finish up 26
Encore 8b, goes back again to finish up 23.
Biceps Dur 8a starts extreme R and finishes up 23.

Up the slope the fine and rather bold **Image In 7a** (gets 7a thanks to bad landing), is the line which crosses the **9B Le Choix des Larmes 6a.**

27 6bW L'Abbatoir 7a Done in 1960! A benchmark 7a. Possible static but most lunge optimistically for the top.
28 L'Hélicoptère 7a Direct to slope from crack of 27, then slap for its jug. You'll see where the name comes from when you fall off.
29 6tW Carnage 7b The classic power problem of the forest and hard for the grade. **Carnazina 7b+.** Start up 29, finish up 30.
30 6qW La Bérézina 7c A classic and a good example of the specificity of some of the hard problems; good conditions and "feeling" help. Normally done with a bizarre toe hook to start but possible without.
31 Bérézina-Carnage 7c+ Up 30 to finish up 29.
32 L'Apothéose 7c+
33 La Balance 7b+ to 8a Another classic with countless methods. The easiest is known affectionately as la Balancette.
34 Cortomaltèse 7a
35 14B Fissure Morin 4+
36 9R La Daubé 6c
37 6W La Défroquée 6c+

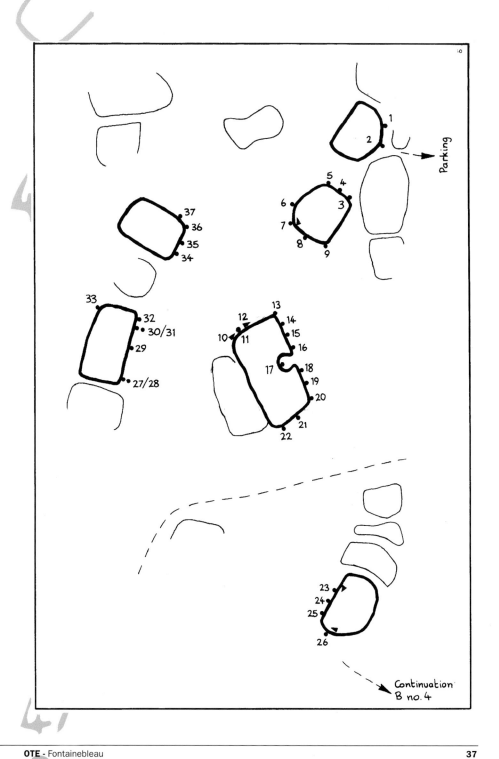

1 Belle de Jour 7a L to R
2 2 fun oranges
3 **7a+** L to R to finish up mushroom holds
4 50 2+
5 Technograte 7b
6 5
7 Clé en Mains 7a
8 30 3-
9 43bB 5-
10 34R 5
11 33R 5+
12 Big Crotte 7a
13 27R Le Quartier d'Orange 5 1m L is 7b
14 44B La Nationale 5- Starts R of 17 and traverses R to finish up weakness just R of these two slab desperates...
15 L'Ange Gardien 7c
16 17W La Super Prestat 7b+ 1.5m L. A landmark slab climb.
  END White
17 500 La Prestat 3+ Done in 1914.
  END Orange.
18 15W La Stalingrad 6b Another milestone, done in 1950. Bold.
19 48B La Paillon Directe 4+/5 The chipped holds are hard to ignore but it's still magnificent. R hand finish slightly harder.
20 32R La Couppel 5+

La Dalle du Baquet
21 30R 6a
22 47B 5
23 31R 5+

24 46B 5-
25 29R 5
Between these two problems you have **11Bl 5** and 45B 4+.
26 28R La Nasser 5+
27 23R 5
28 L'Idiot 7c+ The arete to the L gives a good problem; **L'Angle Obtu 6c**
29 26R 5+
30 25R 5+
31 41B 5
32 31B 3
33 32B 5

34 5+
35 33B 5
36 34B 5+
37 35B 5- The L arete is La Mollissante 6a
38 36B 4+
39 Bisounours 6c
40 ?
41 410 2
42 360 2+
43 30B 4+
44 350 2
45 29B 4+
46 320 3
47 Coup de Feel 8a+ Is this chipped test-piece still possible since a key hold broke?
48 13R 5
49 9Bl 5+
50 28B 5-
51 8Bl Erectissima 6a
52 12R 5

Traverses:
From 49 traverse the entire boulder, 7a.
Les Crampes à Messner 6a R to L from arete by 46, finish up 49

53 27B 4+
54 26B 4
55 330 3-
56 23bB 4
57 17bB 5
58 Plats Toniques 7c
59 17B 4+

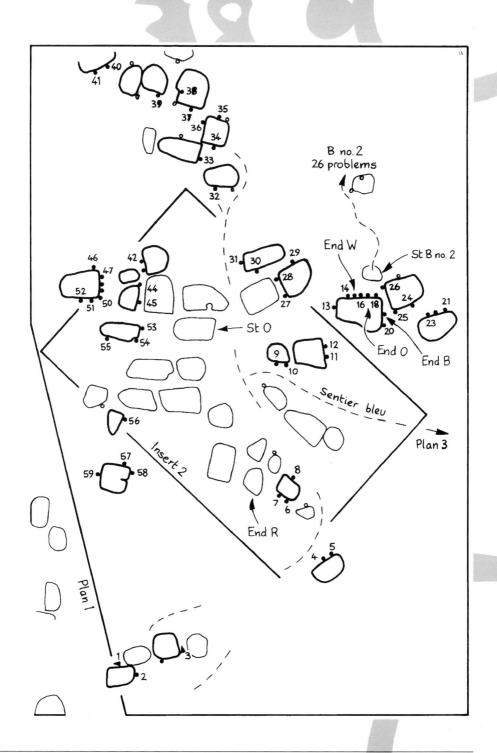

1   Courage Fuyons 7a
2   **Tour de Pise directe 7b**
3   11bW Tour de Pise 6c
4   **20B La Borniol 5**
5   Maison de la Presse 6b
6   **42R La Fauchée 6a**
7   **19B 4+**
8   **Banlieue Nord 7b+** L to R
     Finish R of 9
9   La Menthe à l'Eau 5
10   21B 4+
11   40R 5
12   **Doctor Jones 6b** Very slopey!
13   **39R La Clavicule 5+** The arete to hidden
     hold in scoop. The L wall has 3 unmarked
     reds; 5+/6a
14   **Kilo de Beurre 7a+** L to R Exit up 12 or
     thereabouts. And back 7c
15   41R 5+
16   **10bW La Dix Tractions 6b**
17   **10W La Vie d'Ange 7a**
18   18B 5+
19   **11W La Clé 6c+**
20   22B 5
21   **38R La Bicolore 5+**
22   **35R Les Esgourdes 5**
23   **Digitale 7c+** Despite various broken holds
     this fingery testpiece has kept its grade.
24   **37R La Coupe de Rouge 5+** Just to the L,
     23B 5
25   24B 5-
26   **9tW La Rhume Folle 7a**
27   **9bW L'Enclume 6b+**
28   **9W La Folle 6b**
29   36R 6a
30   La Bouiffe 7a
31   **8W La Forge 6c** A good intro to the harder
     slabs
32   **Super forge 7a**
33   **7W La Résistante 6b** The fine
     groove/arete with a poor landing.
34   **14R Les Bretelles 6b** A good example of
     where a little cunning makes a hard move
     almost straightforward.
35   **340 La Jarretelle 4-**
36   15R 5+

37   **16R La V1 5**
38   **37B L'Angle Authenac 5+**
39   Le Corbillard 6c
40   17R 5 Traverse **La Longue Marche 6c+**
     L to R from 34 to exit up arete R of 40
41   **Golden Feet 8a** Done in 1989 and few
     repeats since, this eliminate epitomises
     hard wall climbing at Bleau. Tiny holds
     that may leave you without fingernails.
42   **Lune de Fiel 7c+** As above
43   38B 5+
44   **18R La Parrallèle 5+**
45   **19R La Leineinger 5+**
46   **20R La Suzanne 5+**
47   **39B La Porthos 5-**
48   La Marco 6b+
49   **21R La Nescafé 6a**
50   2-   START Orange
51   **12W La Chicorée 6c**
52   Jean Jiskan 5
53   **10Bl Le Nez 6a**
54   40B 5
55   **22R La Marie Rose 6a** Done in 1946, this
     was the first official 6a in the forest.
56   43B 4+
57   **14W Le Quatrième Angle 6c**
58   Cornemuse 7b+
59   **24R La Troisième arête 5+** Between 59
     & 60; Pas la Peine, an eliminate 7b
60   **42B 5**
61   **13W La Joker 7a** First climbed in 1953!

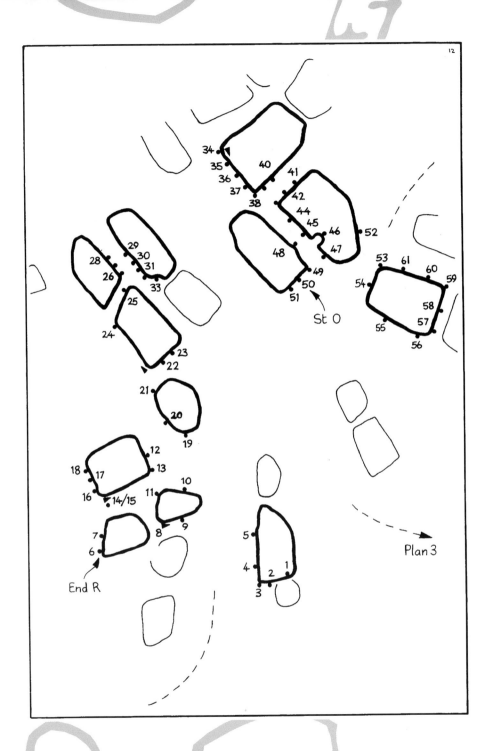

St O

End R

Plan 3

The following problems are, almost without exception, excellent. Always quiet.

1 **14Bl Durandal 5+** 1.5m R is 5 3m R is 6b

2 15Bl La Vipère 6a Just L is Grosse Casse 6b+

3 **16Bl La Brioche 6a** The superb steep arete.

4 17Bl La Fissure Rolland 5+

5 23Bl Le Sentier Bleu 5

6 5+

7 **22Bl La Digitale (aka la Fissure du Crocodile) 5+** The thin crack.

8 21bBl Violence morale 6c

9 21Bl 6a Start up 7 and traverse L

10 **19Bl La Francis 5-**

11 20Bl La Trivellini 6a

12 **22bBl Le Bivouac 6c** Upside down fun, as is...

13 **22tBl Le Bivouac Direct 7a+**
Expo en Ciel 7b+ L to R to exit extreme R.

14 25Bl La Psyssure 6b

15 **26Bl La Mummery 6b**

16 **28tBl Festin de Pierres 7a**

17 28Bl La Philou 5+

18 Zone Erogène 7a+ Behind this there are 2 traverses; On a Volé le Frisbee 7b (?) and on the other side of the gravel path, in a corridor, **Les Pieds Nickés 7c+**

19 Zouk Machine 6c+

20 Scareface (crack) L side 5+ R side 6a+

21 Roxanne 6b The R of 3 marked lines

22 27Bl 5+

23 Angel Face 7b

24 3 different L to R traverses start here; Radio Corbeau, 7a goes R to an exit before 25, **Les Petits Anges 7b+** continues to finish up 26 and... **Sina qua non, 8a** exits up 27. Butch!

25 **30Bl Le Carré d'As 6c** Old (1950), bold and rarely repeated. The bald rib moving L. Maybe worth a brush.

26 **29Bl Duroxmanie 6c.** Start at jug on L. You must do this! Unnecessary chipped hold at top. The direct is 7a+.

27 **29bBl Michel Ange 7b+** *Very* powerful. Naughty chipped foothold is allowed.

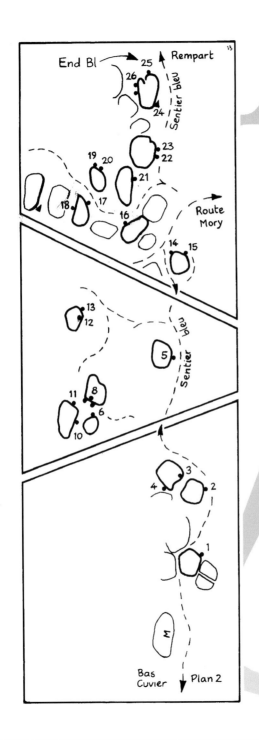

DIRECTIONS

Park as for Bas Cuvier. From the car park nearest the boulders, follow the broad track (Route Mory) which cuts off to the R, for about 400ms, then turn L into a clearing. At the back R hand side of this clearing, you'll find tucked away in amongst the blocs the superb boulder of Le Carré d'As, Duroxmanie and Michel Ange (see Bas Cuvier plan 3). The Sentier bleu cuts across the clearing and up the hillside from here, leading you in a couple of minutes into the heart of Cuvier Rempart. Alternatively follow the sentier bleu from Bas Cuvier.

CHARACTER

Despite the proximity of the N7, Rempart has a certain mountain feel about it. It is very rarely, if ever busy. The jumble of large blocs, which squat on the side of the ridge, can be rather confusing on first aquaintance. The southern part dries quickly after rain. The rest tend to stay humid and therefore dangerous.

CLIMBING

Red AD- (16 probs)
Yellow D- (13 probs)
Black ED- (47 probs)

In 1947 the first circuit in the forest was traced here. It was conceived as a training circuit for the Alps. Nearly 50 years later, Cuvier Rempart hosts some of Fontainebleau's finest hard problems, including the classic quartet of Big Boss, Fourmis Rouges, Tristesse and Big Golden and one of the hardest straight up (or in this case straight out) problems in the forest; Fatman. Many of the problems are either high or have poor landings or both, so it pays to come with a good spotter and/or a crashmat. Even the two 'easy' circuits demand a cool head at times. Nearly half of Rempart's problems are unmarked. One of them, the classic Angle Allain (5+), was way ahead of its time when it was first climbed in 1934. Sixty-one years later, it's still bloody desperate! Sadly some of the more obscure problems are being lost to the lichen through lack of traffic. The quiet north side of the plateau is well worth exploring.

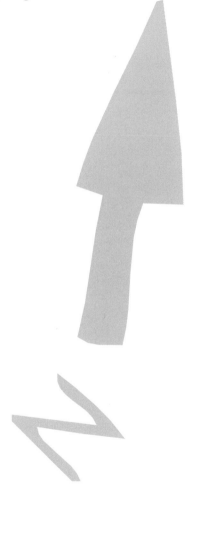

1   1Bl 4+   START Black
2   **Massacre au Supermarché 7c** L to R to arete. And back, 8b
3   **El Zopilote 6c**
4   La Philippine 6b
5   Babouchka 6b
6   Tico Tico 7a
7   L'Aérotilt 5+
8   **10Y 4**
9   **Gabonis 7b**
10 **Histoire sans Fin 6c**
11 **11Y 4**
12 2Bl 5-
13 3Bl 5+
14 5Bl 5+
15 **7Bl 5**
16 Le Kick 6b
17 Les Nouvelles Ecritures 7a
18 5Y 4
19 6Bl 5
20 **T Rex 7c+** Hard for the grade.
21 9Bl 5+
22 **C'était Demain 8a** Forest's 1st 8a
23 **Septième Ciel 6c** A neglected gem

24 Jeux de Nous 6c
25 Boogle Chaise 6c
26 12Bl 5+
The Big Four. A crash pad, an army of spotters or the ability to bounce advisable.
27 **Big Boss 7b+** Slightly spoilt by the adjacent boulder but still a classic.
28 **Fourmis Rouges 7c/7c+** Enough time to read a short novel in a fall from the crux.
29 **Tristesse 7c** Some jump off after the crux, avoiding the easier but high finishing moves, and then claim an ascent. But in their hearts they know...
30 **Big Golden 7c+** Not as high as FR but a bad landing makes repeats rare. Hard for the grade.
31 Anglissimo 6a
32 1Y 3+   START Yellow
33 **Durane Durane 6c**
34 **Green Peace 6c**
35 12Y 3+
36 Pirlouit 5+
37 Johan 6b
38 Immodium 7a

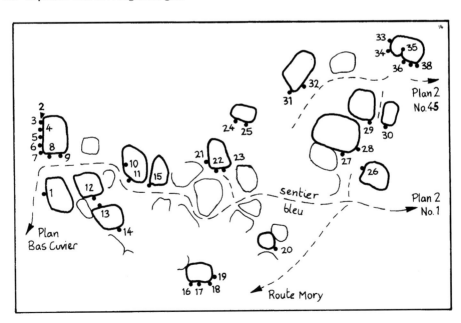

1   Fatman 8b? Repeated at last in November '96 by Sebastien Frigault. Hopeful candidates note: it does not start right from the back of the roof. Gourmandise 8a+ climbs the roof just to the R, starting slightly further back. Traverses L at lip to exit up Fatman.
2   Ticket Choc 6a
3   La Tête de Veau 6a
4   Ticket Chic 5+
5   4R 3
6   **19B La Haut le Pied 5+**
7   **La Minute Nécessaire de M. Cyclopède 7c** R to L to finish up 5 ...and back **8b**

8   **La Décibel 6c**
9   **La Merci Dieu 6c**
10 18Bl 5
11 L'Intruse 5+
12 5R 3+
13 Le Baptème de l'Air 7c
14 La Mandale 5+
15 22Bl 5
16 **Digitibus 7a** Just to the R, 6b
17 Tacotac 6c
18 24Bl 5+
19 25Bl 5
20 Choc Délice 6a
21 **Où are you 7a+**
22 **Baisers Volés 7c**
23 **Haute Tension 7c+** L hand exit   Direct is **Hyper Tension 8a**   Also here; **Le Miroir des Vanités** L to R 8b, and back 8b+. R to L and back 8c? Another typically fingery JP Bouvier horror and a candidate for the hardest bit of climbing in the forest. Sica was used to reinforce some holds. Shame.
24 Tif et Tondu 6b
25 Le Golgotha 7a
26 **28Bl 5**
27 La Grogon de Bluxte 6c
28 Kanata 6b
29 29Bl 4+
30 31Bl 6a
31 Orn 5
32 Le Coeur 6b

33 35Bl 4+
34 34Bl 4+
35 **La Grande Arête 5+**
36 **La Souveraine 6b** Just L is Peau Lisse en Péril 7b+
37 Professional Killer 7a+ Up and L
38 L'Envolée Perverse 6b
39 Expin Expo 5+
40 Jazz Volant 5+
41 **Laser 6c**
42 Le Poucet 5+ (without arete)
43 **L'Angle Allain (east) 6a**
44 **L'Angle Allain (north) 5+**
45 43Bl 5
46 La Rescapée 6a
47 37Bl 5-
48 Malheur aux Vaincus 6a
49 Video Clip 6b Traverse

The following problems are on the north side of the Rempart and deserve more attention...
50 Sortie d'Enfer 6b
51 **Salathé Wall 7a+**
52 **Black Magic 6b**
53 **L'Angle Obtus 7a**
54 15R 3-
55 **La Double Arête 5+**
56 L'Ouvreur Inconnu 6c
57 **Philanthropie 7a**
58 Cadeau de Consolation 6a
59 14R 3
60 **L'Emeraude 7b**
61 **Association de Bienfaiteurs 6a**

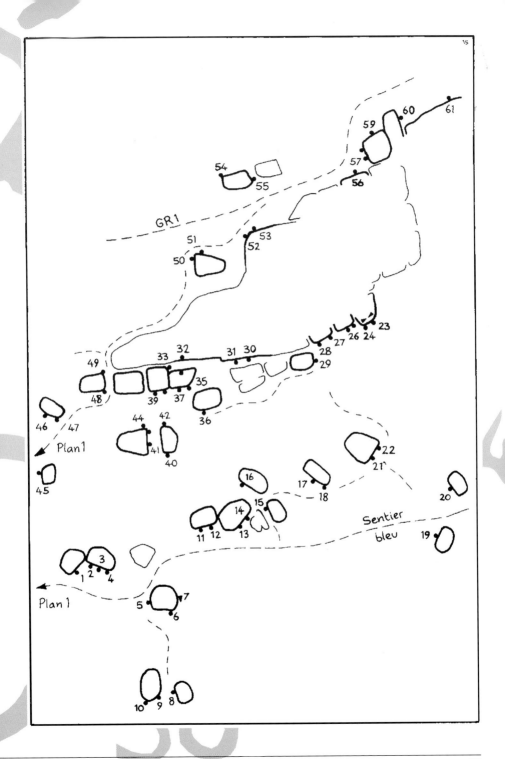

LA MERVEILLE

DIRECTIONS

As for Rempart, but follow le Route Mory for an additional 500ms, turning L at the second turning. About 100ms after this, La Merveille is on the R. Alternatively you can follow the sentier bleu from Bas Cuvier passing through Cuvier Rempart. It passes alongside La Merveille.

CHARACTER

Otherwise known as "Le bloc aux mille visages" (the bloc of a thousand faces), la Merveille is in a beautiful setting but dries slowly after rain.

CLIMBING

What a boulder! And a sure way to escape the hordes at Bas Cuvier. Only 10 or so problems but well worth a visit. Hard, technical and off-vertical for the most part. Despite good landings, it's disconcertingly high, so a top-roping bolt has been placed at the top.

1   Le Surplomb 6c
2   Garcymore 3
3   Le Sourire de Denise 5
4   Les Colonnes 6b
5   Le Sourire de David 7a You can perhaps do Abattoir in Dachsteins and roller skates but you won't necessarily manage this fine, rarely repeated slab testpiece. Illustrates perfectly the gap between 'slab' grades and the rest. Starts below the arete before pulling R onto the wall.
6   **7a** R hand variant of above, joining it halfway
7   La Fissure 6a
8   L'Epaule 7a
9   La Dalle de Fer 7c
10   L'Arête 6a

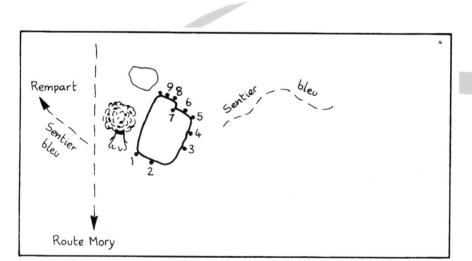

...everything
you need
for

Fontainebleau..

PEAK DISTRICT
Main Road
Hathersage
S32 1BB
01433
651936

SNOWDONIA
High Street
Llanberis
LL55 4EN
01286
871534

MAIL ORDER
VISA
VISA DELTA
MASTERCARD
SWITCH
ELECTRON

SHEFFIELD
by The Foundry
45, Mowbray St
S3 8EN
0114
2797427

...probably

Climbing Photos © Tim Hulley

E-MAIL
OUT-SIDE@OUT-SIDE.DEMON.CO.UK

DIRECTIONS
Just west of Cuvier is the extremely chic village of Barbizon, normally reached via the N37 from the north or the D409 from the south. Follow its main street eastwards and continue straight on until you reach a large crossroads (which can also be reached from the small road that leaves from the Bas Cuvier car park).

From here go straight on for car park 4 and Envers d'Apremont (plan 8). Turn R for carparks 1, 2 and 3. Car park 3 and Apremont Bizons (plans 9 and 10) are straight on where the road trends L. For les Gorges d'Apremont, carparks 1 and 2 (plans 1 to 7) are a little further on the L.

CHARACTER
Les Gorges d'Apremont Popular but so spread out that it's always possible to find calm. Dries quickly but can get very hot in summer.

L'Envers d'Apremont Quiet and slow drying. Fine spot for summer evenings.

Apremont Bizons Quiet and slow drying.

CLIMBING
Les Gorges d'Apremont
White (children's 43 problems) Well marked and fun.

Yellow PD+ (42 problems) Excellent beginner's circuit

2 Oranges no.3 AD (46 problems) and no.1 AD+ (28 problems) Nowhere desperate, some beautiful problems, but some appalling landings will intimidate the inexperienced climber.

2 Blues no.5 D (44 problems) and no.13 D (40 problems) Varied and technical.

Red (aka Fraise écrasée) no.4 D+/TD- (32 problems) Old, neglected classic.

Salmon TD (74 problems) Long, spread out and erratic (3 to 6a). Some fine problems.

Light Blue ED- (35 problems) Conceived as a crack climbing circuit. Wide ranging in terms of difficulty (4 to 7a), it has some superb problems, some extremely esoteric.

2 Reds no.10 TD+ (40 problems) and no.12

ED- (46 problems) These give a stern test of technique in the fifth grade with a few sixes thrown in for good measure.

White ED+ (14 problems) Classic hard circuit where all bleausard techniques are neccesary for success.

L'Envers d'Apremont
Orange AD (45 problems) Good traditional circuit with lots of intermediate boulders. The start is tricky to find but you can join it at the no.16 (next to la Fissure des Alpinistes) see below and map.

Red TD- (50 problems) Excellent but neglected circuit.

Apremont Bizons
Orange AD+ (48 problems)

Red TD- (43 problems)

Le Désert d'Apremont
2 Yellows, 3 Oranges and a Blue.

And marked on the map...
(Strong) trainspotters must not overlook...

1 **Tempête 7c+** L to R traverse next to Barbizon, just below the crest of the ridge, look hard! Typically Fontainebleau, there are no holds really, the boulder is just one enormous sloper. Must be COLD!

More amenable, next to the 16 orange at l'Envers d'Apremont...

2 **La Fissure des Alpinistes 5** Done in 1934 by Pierre Allain, an essential tick for history lovers.

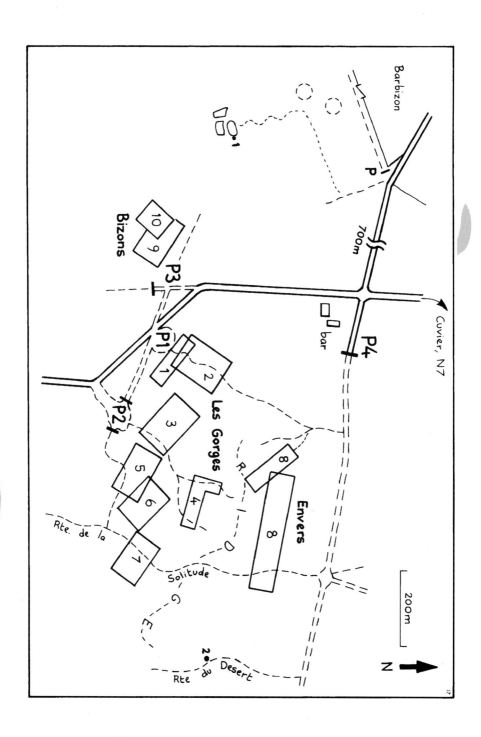

1 **57S 4+** This is also the descent or leap to adjacent boulder.

2 **1R 5+**   START Red no. 10

3 **2R 6c**

This boulder, big by Fontainebleau standards, has four fine microroutes and a chain for the descent...

4 **3R 6a** Superb but graded for height not difficulty.

5 **30 Jeu de Ficelle 3+** Wobblers common on the 'holdless' exit...

6 **56S 5** Scary finish.

7 **7a+** This takes the weakness by the chain.

8 **5R 5+**

9 **55S 5**

10 56S 4

11 60 2

12 **50 3**

13 40 4

14 5+/6a

15 **20 3**

16 53S 4

17 10 3   START Orange no. 3

18 100 3+

19 7R 5

20 8R 5+

21 **11R 5+**

22 **52S 4**

23 Rv 3

24 13R 5+

25 136R 5+

26 9R 5+

27 10R 5+

28 **130 4**

29 **17R 5**   L side of arete 6a

30 150 2+

31 160 3

32 170 3

33 19R 5

34 140 2

35 180 4

36 Small, overhanging, chipped groove

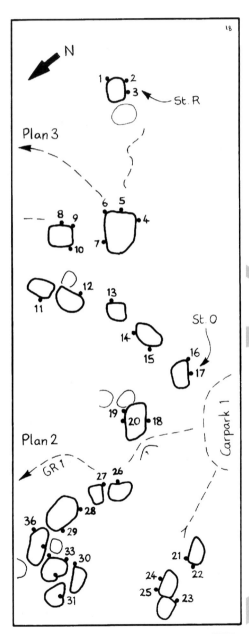

Philippe le Denmat on La Super Prestat
7b+, Cuvier. Alain Hoffman

1 190 2+
1a Heiroglyph 7a
1b L is **Jolie Môme 7c+** R is 6b
2 200 3
3 20R 5 L to R and up
4 230 2+
5 240 3-
6 250 3-
7 260 3+
8 210 4-
9 220 2
10 21R 5
11 270 Le Promenoir 3+
12 23R 5
13 22R 5+
14 290 2+
15 300 3-
16 340 3
17 350 3+
18 310 3-
19 3203+
20 330 3
21 25R 5+
22 26R 5 R to L and up. Direct is fun.
23 360 3+ 36b0 4+
24 370 4-
25 27R 5
26 380 4- 38b 4- 38t 4
27 390 3+
28 A typical piece of Apremont esoterica; down in the hole there's a good **7a** and various games.
29 400 3
30 28R 5+
31 29R 5
32 30R 5+
33 420 4-
34 410 3- 41b 41t 4
35 32R 5+
36 31R 5-
37 33R 5-
38 430 3+
39 37R 4+
40 38R 5
41 410 3-
42 35R 5

43 36R 5+
44 450 4-
45 40R 5+   END Red no. 10
46 460 Le Mot de la Fin 3+
The arete to the L is **46b 4-**
                              END Orange no. 3

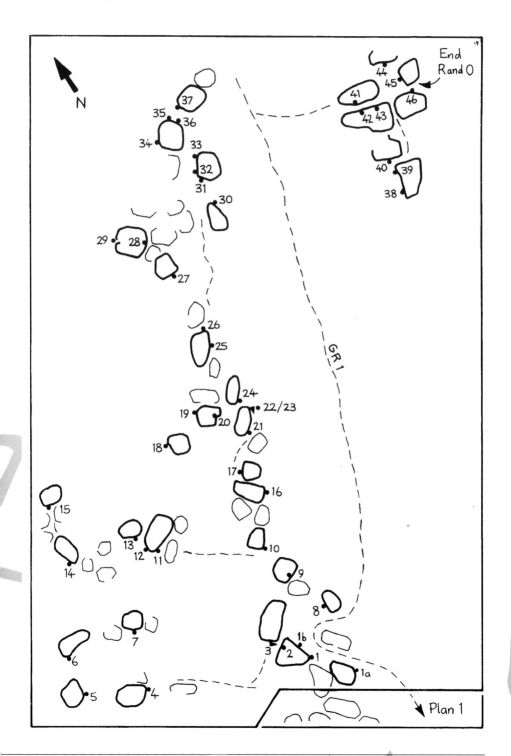

From car park 2 take the L hand track. The problems begin within a few metres.

1 1Bb 4-
2 1B 3+ START Blue no. 5
3 2B 3
4 3B 4
5 4B 3
6 5B 3+
7 3W 1
8 6B 4
9 7B 4-
10 8B 3+
11 9B 3+
12 W R to L Finish L of 11
13 10B 3+
14 74S 4+ END Salmon no. 6
15 73S 4
16 13LB Le Rince Dalle 5 Crack + L to R
17 2S 4+
18 1S 5 START Salmon no. 6
19 41Y 2+
20 19B 4-
21 42Y 3-
22 18B 3+
23 12LB Lamentations 7a Steep, thin slab.
24 17B 3+
25 72S 5-
26 13B 4+
27 12B 4
28 71S 5-
29 15B 3+
30 9LB 5 L to R and up
31 96LB L'Adrénaline 7a Bold
Between 31 and 32 is 6c
32 16B 4+
33 24B 3+
34 23B 3+
35 69S 4+
36 22B 4
37 68S 4+
38 20B 4-
39 7a R to L to finish up 42
Three excellent unmarked problems...
40 6b
41 6b+
42 6c Légitime Adhérence Bizarre start, bold

finish.
43 21B 4+
44 67S 5
45 6a+
46 66S 5+
47 28B 4-
48 29B 3+
49 5LB La Bagatelle 4-
50 4LB L'Effet Yau de Poêle 4
51 27B 3+
52 25B 4
53 8bLB 4+
54 8LB L'Empire des Sens 6a The hideous cleft
55 26B 4-
56 7LB Le Gibbon 5+ L to R
57 6LB Le Toit Tranquille 7a Esoteric and rarely done. Good but awkward jams to a nasty exit.
58 Faux Contact 7b/7c+ depending on the method
59 W
60 58S 4
61 59S 4+
62 33B 4
63 32B 4
64 34B 4
65 2LB Le Poultiquet 5+
2bLB Le Poulpe 6c moving L
66 37B 4
67 1LB L'Esprit du Continent 5+ Bold
68 Une Idée en l'Air 7b Start as for 67 but move R to climb the weakness in the superb wall.
69 48S 5+ The bold slab
70 Le Croque Mitaine 5+
START Light Blue no. 11
71 Two problems here; **Marginal 7b+** goes up, trending L to finish. Another problem **7a+/b** goes up and slightly R.
72 38B 4
73 39B 3+
74 40B 3
75 41B 4
76 42B 4-
77 43B 4
78 44B 4- END Blue no. 5

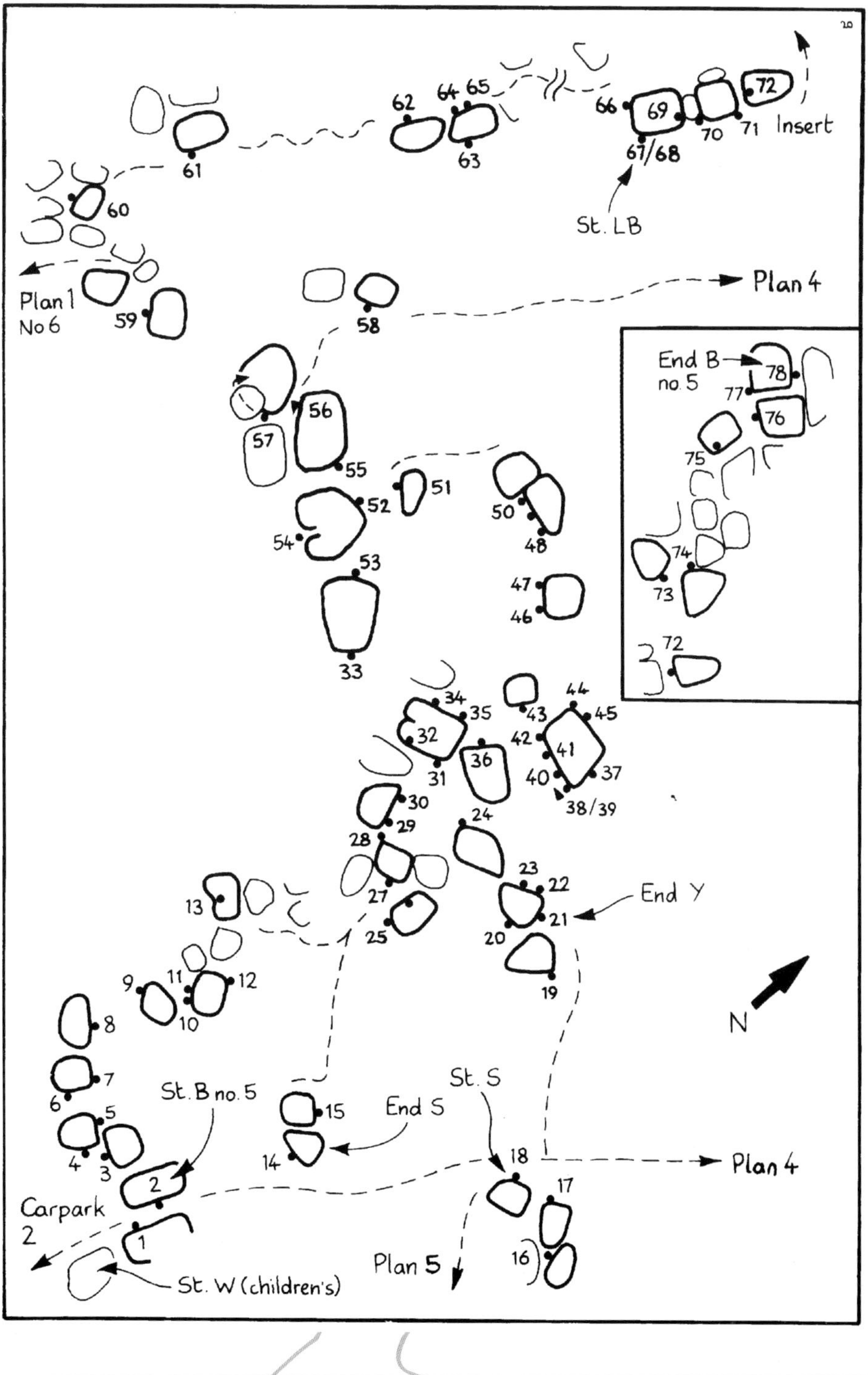

Insert
St. LB
Plan 4
Plan 1
No 6
End B
no. 5
End Y
N
St. B no. 5
St. S
End S
Plan 4
Carpark
2
Plan 5
St. W (children's)

Antisocial? You won't see a soul up here. The problems deserve more traffic...

1   45S 4
2   46S 3+
3   47S 5+
4   44S 5-
5   43S 5+
6   42S 4-
7   41S 4
8   40S 4-
9   39S 4-
10 38S 4+
11 37S 5
12 36S 4
13 35S 4-

To continue the Salmon circuit (in reverse), head straight up the hill on the other side of the path from no.35. At the crest of the ridge trend right and you'll get to 46R (37 plan 6) with 34S just beside it.

Plan 6 – Up to crest of ridge – turn R

Plan 3

13

12

11

10

9

8

7

6

5

4

3

Plan 8

2

1

Plan 3

Plan 3

High

mountain | sports

always there when you get it by post

To receive High through your letterbox each month, simply complete the coupon below or telephone on 01536 525550 (24hrs) £30 (UK) or £36 (Overseas) for 12 issues.

To include £36.00 BMC membership when you subscribe to High (UK only).

I authorise you to debit my Access/Visa/Mastercard account with the amount of £..................
My Card No. is ☐☐☐☐ ☐☐☐☐ ☐☐☐☐ ☐☐☐☐
Expiry Date..................
Cardholder's name and address (if different form delivery address)

....

....

*CREDIT CARDS MAKE OVERSEAS SUBSCRIPTIONS EASY

Please arange .... subscriptions to High Starting with the next issue plus BMC MEMBERSHIP £36.00 Yes/No(UK subscribers only).
I enclose my remittance *for £..............payable to High Magazine Ltd.
NAME (Caps)..
DELIVERY ADDRESS (Caps)..

....

Send to: HIGH MAGAZINE, GreenShires Publishing, Telford Way, Kettering, Northants NN16 8UN, UK

From car park 2, take the righthand track, passing the start of the yellow circuit at the barrier and a few good problems on the R hand bloc. A short walk along the main path brings you to the first problems...

1 **4R Le Piano a Queue 6a**
2 **3R 5**
3 **2R 5**
4 **1R 5+**   START Red no. 12
5 5R 5- R to L
6 22Y 3-
7 **7S 5**
8 **21Y 3-**
9 26Y 2+
10 **6S 4+**
11 **14LB L'Ostétoscope 5+**
12 12S 4- On the other side of this bloc is a traverse; R to L 6c+ and back 7b
13 11S 5
14 **8S 5-**
15 **G**
16 **BI**
17 6R 5+
18 **9S 5+**
19 10S 4+
20 3W 6b L to R to mantle. Another traverse goes R from R arete to exit round the corner 6b+/6c+
21 6a L to R
22 **G**
23 **7b L to R**
24 17LB L'Across en l'Air 4+
25 **G**
26 **2bW La Médaille en Chocolat 7a** (direct to boss at top)
27 **7R Les Crampes à Mémère 6a** R to L and up
28 18LB L'Astrolabe 5 L to R
29 **1W Hyper Plomb 6c/7a** Exit direct or easier, slightly R.   START White
30 **2W Le Dromadaire 7b**
31 **14S 5-**
32 21LB Le Pont Mirabeau 5
33 8R 5
34 15S 4+
35 4W La Dalle du Toboggan 6a
36 **9R Toboggan 5**

37 10R 5
38 R variant 5+
39 **11R Les Yeux 6a**
40 **12R Le Château de Sable 5+**
41 15R 5+
42 5W L'Ebréchée 6c
43 23LB Ignès 6a
44 **22LB La Super Simca 5**
45 13R Durandal 5+
46 18S 4+
47 **14R La Rampe 5+**
48 **10W La Lune 6c/7a**
49 16LB La Michodière 5
50 **34R La Science Friction 5+**
51 15G 3+
52 **15LB Les Fesses à Simon 5+**
53 17O 3-
54 38R 5+
55 37R 5+
56 **13W La Tarentule 6c**
57 12W L'Arc d'Héraclès 6c
58 35R 5+ 36R 6a L to R
59 28S 4+
60 1B 4+   START Blue no. 13
61 **19O Les Verrues 2+**
62 25S 6a
63 18G
64 33R 5+
65 **20O Le Paquet 4**
66 **9W Le 13ème Travail d'Hercule 6c+** Normally done with a crafty mix of toe jams and heel hooks but also goes from the back of the roof without. Classic.
67 **24S La Balafre 6a** Big slab
68 **31bLB Surplomb de l'Avocat 5**
69 **Fleur de Rhum 7a+**
70 32LB La Mélodie Juste 5+
71 **32bLB Le Soupir 7a**
72 **32R La Psycho 6b**
73 33LB Le Piano Vache 5
74 **21O L'Escalier Dérobé 3+**
75 2B 4

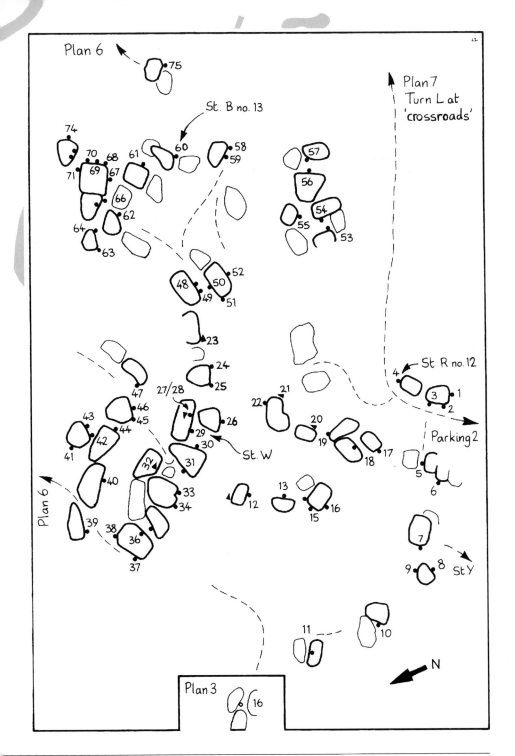

Plan 6

75

Plan 7
Turn L at
'crossroads'

St. B no. 13

74
70 68 61 60 58
71 69 67 59
66
62
64 63

57
56
54
55 53

48 52
50
49 51

23

24
25

St R no. 12

47
43 46
45
41 42 44
40
39 38 36
37

27/28
26
29
30
31
32
33
34

St. W

21
22
20
19
18 17
13
12
15 16

4
3 1
2

Parking 2

5
6

7
9 8 St Y

11
10

Plan 6

N

Plan 3
16

1   16R 5
1b 17R 5+
1c 18R 5+
2   6W La Ténébrante 6b/c
3   27O L'Inventaire 3+
3a 7a
4   24LB La Salamandre 5+
5   25LB La Vie Lente 5+
28R La Conque 6a Just R of 5
6   28O 3   END Orange no.1
7   29R L'Ancien 5+
8   30R La Valse 5
9   31R La Que Faire 5+
10 19S 5-
11 35LB La Sortie des Artistes 6a
             END Light Blue no.11
12 34LB Le Surplomb à Coulisse 5+
13 8W La Conque 6c
14 23O 2
15 24O 3
16 20S 6a
17 24R Les Verrues 6b
18 25R 5-
19 28LB Icare 5
20 21S 5-
21 26R La Claque 5
22 26O 4+
23 26LB La Muse Hermétique 5+
24 27LB L'Angle Obtus 5+
25 20R Le Coin Pipi 5-
26 21R 5-
27 22S 5
28 23S 5-
29 7W L'Oeuf 6c
30 22R Le Baiser Vertical 5
31 23R 5
32 15O 4-
33 14W Les Lames 6c   END White
34 33S 5+
35 21B L'Arythmie 5-
36 34S 4-
37 46R Le John Gill 5 L to R + roof
             END Red no.12
38 22B 4
39 32S 4-
40 23B 4

41 12O 3+
42 20B La Fissure Diabolique 4+
43 19B 4-
44 10O 4+
45 18B 4
46 17B 4+
47 31S 5-
48 29LB Le Merle Noir 5
49 44R 4+
50 8O 3-
51 14B 3+
52 16B 4
53 15B 4+
54 13B 4
55 12B 4-
56 29bLB L'Adieu aux Armes 5
57 30LB La Gnôse 5
To the R on the next bloc is **L'Alchimiste 8b.**
58 3B 4-
59 4B 4-
60 31LB La Clepsydre 5-
61 5B 4+
62 7a The arete starting on the R and swinging L.
63 6O 3
64 11B 5-
65 42R L'Alternative 5+
66 3O 3 L to R
67 8B L'Oreille à Napo 4
Arete to R is 5. R again is a good hard problem to slope.
68 30S 5
69 7B 4-
70 29S 5+
71 41R L'Arrache Bourse 6a
72 2O 3+   START Orange no. 1
73 39R 6a
74 40R Le Grand Pilier 5+
75 11B 5-
76 12B L'Enfantement 4-

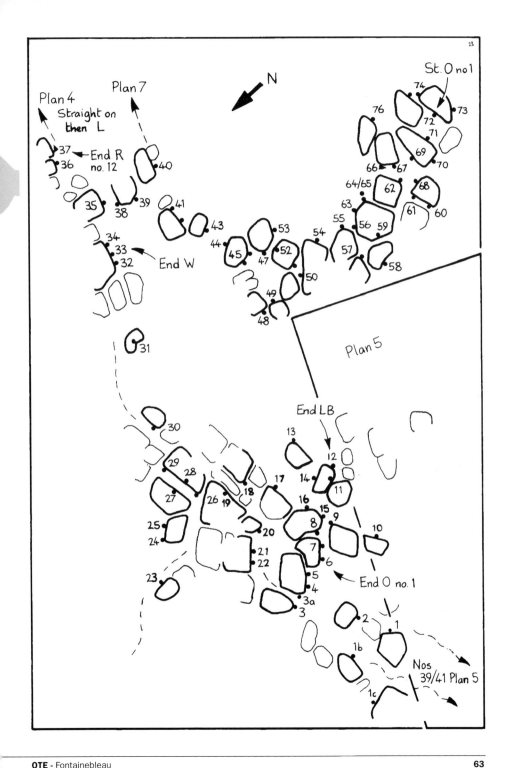

The following problems are undeservedly neglected...

FE stands for fraise écrasée, the no.4 red circuit.

1   24B 5-
2   B
3   25B 3+
4   26B 4
5   27B 4
6   28B 4
7   **29B 5** L to R
8   30B 3+
9   32B 4
10 **33B 4+ L to R**
11 **32FE Le Phallus 5** Named after a long disappeared piece of graffiti.
                                    END FE no. 4
12 37B 4-
13 30FE 4
14 **31FE 5-**
15 36B 4-
16 35B 4-
17 34B 4
18 **37B 4+**
19 6c+ Fun double dyno for slope
20 38B 3+
21 **39B 4+**   END Blue no. 13
22 1FE 4   START FE no. 4
23 1bFE 4-
24 2FE 3+
25 3FE 4-
26 **4FE 4-**
27 5FE 4+ 5b 4+ just to the L
28 **6FE 4** L to R, continue onto next bloc and downclimb arete to finish on ground by red dots.
29 7FE 4-
30 **8FE 5-** both bis are **4+**
31 9FE 4-
32 10FE 5-
33 **11FE 5**
34 12FE 4-
35 13FE 4-
36 **14FE 4**
37 15FE 4-
38 16FE 4

39 17FE 4+
40 **18FE 4**
41 19FE 4-
42 **20 FE 5** L to R
43 **6c** Direct from start of 42. Harder than it looks. Crafty footwork helps.
44 21FE 4 L to R
45 **22FE 4- 22b 4-**
46 23FE 4+
47 24FE 3+
48 **25FE 5**
49 25bFE 6a
50 26FE 4+
51 27FE 4
52 28FE 4
53 **29FE 4+** R hand finish **5-**

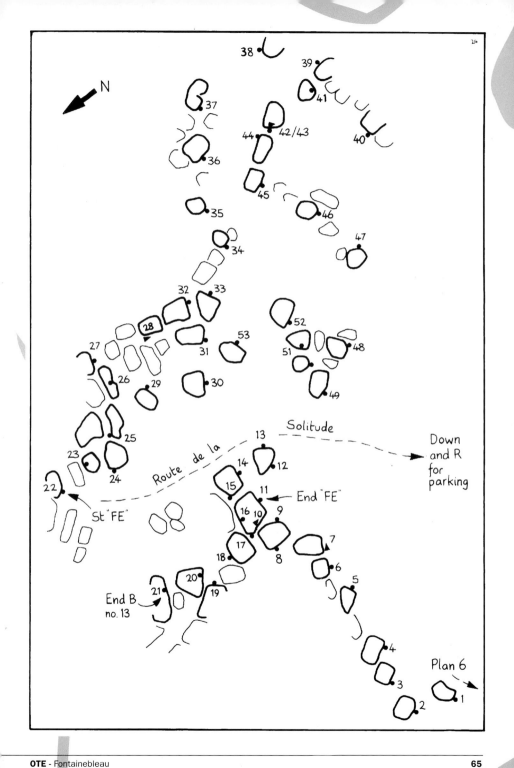

This is the no.1 red circuit, long and spread out, with excellent, varied climbing in a peaceful setting. An excellent spot for a summer evening. From carpark 4 pass the barrier and continue for about 100ms until an obvious R turn. Follow this for a short distance and take the L fork where the path splits. Cut diagonally up the hillside to the L almost immediately (you may spot a red dot on one of the boulders) to reach the start of the circuit.

NB: The second half of the circuit is drawn to a smaller scale.

1 3+
2 5+ L'Enclume
3 4
4 4-
5 5-
6 6- Voyage au bout de l'Envers
7 4+
8 5- Mac Wall
9 5- Bicolor
10 4+
11 4
12 4+ A Tes Souhaits
13 5-
14 4
15 5
16 5+ L'Aspirant Ticket
17 5+
18 4-
19 4
20 4
21 4+
22 5+ Jetman
23 5 Mac Prout
24 5 Dalle de l'Oubli
25 4+
26 5+ Gaz à tous les Etages
27 5
28 4+
29 4
30 5- Le Fil du Grès
31 4+
32 5
33 4-
34 4+
35 4
36 4+
37 4+
38 5+ Cul de Cafard
39 5+ Opposite this is a fine crack **6b**
40 5 Les Vérins
41 4+
42 5- La Fente au Cochon
43 4
44 5+ Chacrotage
45 6- L'Incorruptible
46 5
47 5-
48 4+ La Raie au Porc
49 4+
50 5- Just L **6b**
50m south is an obvious pillar... **Deux Temps Trois Mouvements 6c**

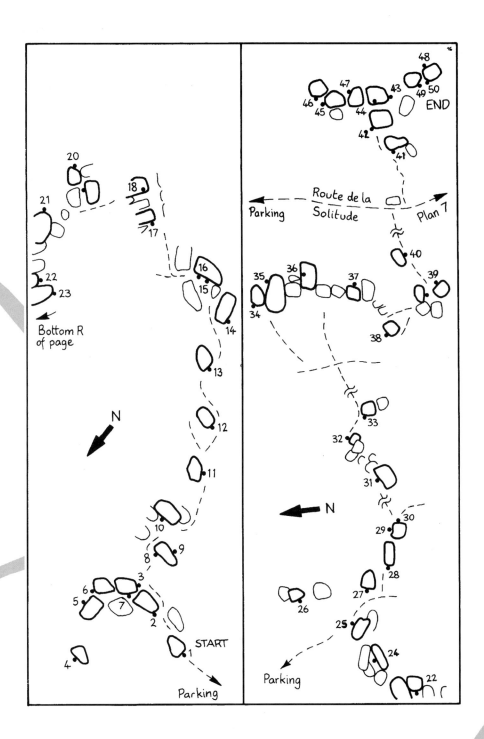

Yet another quiet spot which deserves more attention.

1	10 3+	START Orange no. 3
2	**1R 4**	START Red no. 1
3	20 3+	
4	**2R 5- 2b 5+**	
5	40 4-	
6	30 3-	
7	3R 4	
8	60 3	
9	4R 4+	
10	90 3	
11	80 2	
12	100 4+	
13	**5R 5**	
14	7R 4+	
15	**6R 5-**	
16	8R 4+	
17	120 3	
18	110 3+	
19	6R 5-	
20	**9R 5**	9b 6a Cont. R to finish up 22
21	140 2+	
22	**10R 4+**	
23	11R 4+	
24	150 4+	
25	170 3+	
26	14R 4+	
26a	**La Cave Nicolas 7a**	
27	240 4+ 24b 2+	
28	13R 5-	13b L to R to finish up 13R
29	12R 4+	
30	260 3-	
31	280 4+	
32	270 3+	
33	320 4	
34	310 3+	Just behind, 290 3-
35	300 3+	
36	220 3	
37	15R 5	
38	22b0 3+	
39	210 3-	
40	190 4-	
41	200 4-	
42	17R 4-	
43	**18R 5 18b 6b** 19R 4+	
44	20R 4-	
45	21R 4+	
46	**22R 5-**	
47	23R 4+	
48	24R 4-	
49	**25R 4+ 25b 4**	
50	26R 5	
51	27R	
52	28R	
53	29R	

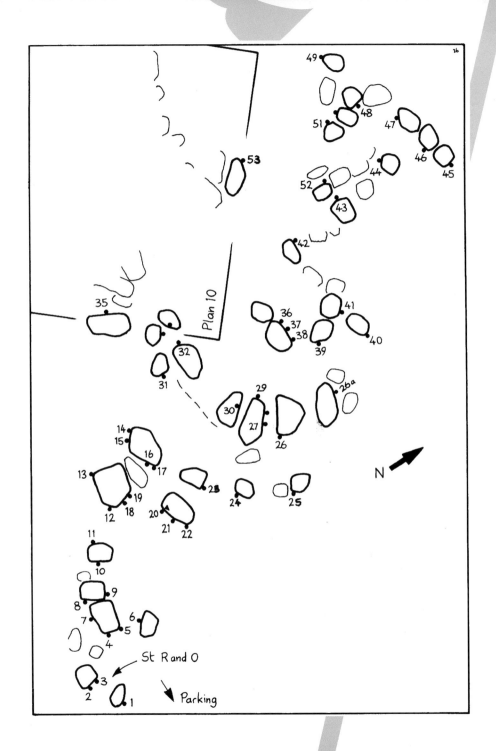

Plan 10

N

St R and O

Parking

1 **36R 6a** L to R and slab to finish
2 **480 3-**   END Orange no. 3
3 37R 4+
4 Rb 4+
5 390 2+
6 **30R 6a** L to R Step down to finish
7 31R 4
8 420 4-
9 32R 4
10 430 2
11 33R 4 33b 4+
12 34bR 4+
13 34R 4+
14 35R 5-
15 470 3
16 **38R 5** 38b 4+
17 39R 4 39b 4+
18 40R 5
19 **41R 5 41b 5/5+**
20 42R 5
21 43R 5-   END Red no. 1

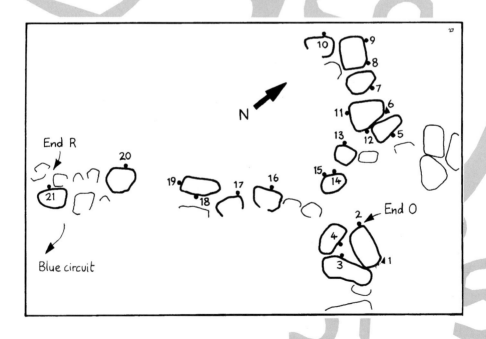

CALVAIRE
DIRECTIONS
From the swimming pool near Fontainebleau station follow the route de la Reine Amélie which contours its way around to an eventual L turn towards la Croix de Calvaire. Parking. Follow the sentier bleu NW and you reach the problems within 150 m.

CHARACTER
Calvaire has one feature, a large roof nick-named the "Calvaire des bras" which stays dry even in the heaviest rain.

CLIMBING
Orange AD (33 problems)
Calvaire is better known for its roof where there are numerous games, strenuous traverses and straight up problems, some of them very hard indeed. The central line through the roof is **Le Toit du Calvaire 6c**. Further L, behind the boulder that marks the start of the orange circuit is the classic **L'Aplat du Gain 8a**.

MONT USSY
DIRECTIONS
Follow the N6 N out of Fontainebleau. At the D116 exit, signposted Fontaine-le-Port come off the N6 and turn L. After about 1km you reach the carrefour du Mont Ussy. Park here. For the circuits, follow the Route du Mont Ussy west for about 400m. They start just R of the path.

CHARACTER
Slow drying and quiet.

CLIMBING
Yellow PD- (28 problems) A pleasant circuit, ideal for beginners.
Orange AD+ (31 problems)
There are also three, for the moment unmarked 'circuits' blue, red and white. The white is ED+ and has some very hard problems.
Le Rocher d'Hercule, which is just east of the carpark has some excellent problems.
The obvious central prow facing the carpark is about **5+** and there are other good but harder problems to either side.

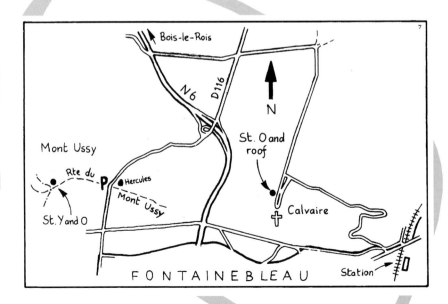

DIRECTIONS

La Cuisinière is found 3kms east of Arbonne-la-Forêt, just south of the D409, the main Fontainebleau/Milly-la-Forêt road. At the eastern end of the long straight east of Arbonne, any one of four closely-spaced turnings will lead you to the car park, situated after about 600m, at the end of the track.

For plans 1, 2 and 3 head diagonally L up the slope from the carpark. For plan 4 head diagonally R, to the R of the middle track.

CHARACTER

This area is well covered with trees and dries more slowly than neighbouring Isatis, particularly the north side of the ridge on plans 1, 2 and 3. Superb atmosphere however and stays fairly cool in hot weather.

CLIMBING

Orange no. 3 (74 problems) The "mountain circuit", a 6km mixture of walking, scrambling and climbing which traces a huge loop around the massif. Easiest access is probably to take the middle path from the carpark for about 125m until a cluster of boulders on the L. The circuit is marked with two orange dashes and the occasional number. Don't get it confused with the short orange circuit in plans 1, 2 and 3.

Orange no.1 (18 problems) Difficult to follow.

Red no.2 D+/TD- Very quiet. Situated SE of the main massif, on the same ridge that the black circuit follows. Start marked on map.

Red no.4 D+/TD- (30 problems)

White ED (48 problems)

Black ED+ (34 problems)

... and some brilliant unmarked problems, some of them extremely hard. Yet another "one of the best massifs in the forest", Cuisinière must be visited. Some of the more obscure problems are well worth the detour but could be overtaken by the inexorable advance of the moss if people don't make the effort. It's worth giving a brush to some of the tops to avoid embarassing wobblers on relatively easy but dirty finishes. Get to it!

And marked on the main Franchard map...

1 **Toutes Peines Confondues 7c** The impressive overhanging prow that wants to be a crack is one of the lines of the forest. Nasty landing and only top roped to date (bolt in place). Virtually ignored since the first ascents. It's on the top of the ridge facing north, just R of a prominent corner crack and opposite the 23R.

2 **Hale Bopp 8a?** BIG dyno, tried by many and first climbed by Fred Nicole in spring '97. Easy to find on the ridge facing southish. Clean cut overhanging wall on crimps way below the top

3 **Le Surplomb de la Coquille 6c** A stone's throw from the main Isatis massif but little known and well hidden. Take a small path that cuts off from beside problem 54 plan 1 as far as la Route des Gorges de Franchard. Turn left and go a few metres before taking a small, easy to miss path that cuts up right. The boulder is up the slope, in a small dip.

4 **Voltane 8a** R to L A brilliant discovery! The final wall is the highlight. It has a couple of worthwhile straight-up problems. Best to park on the D409.

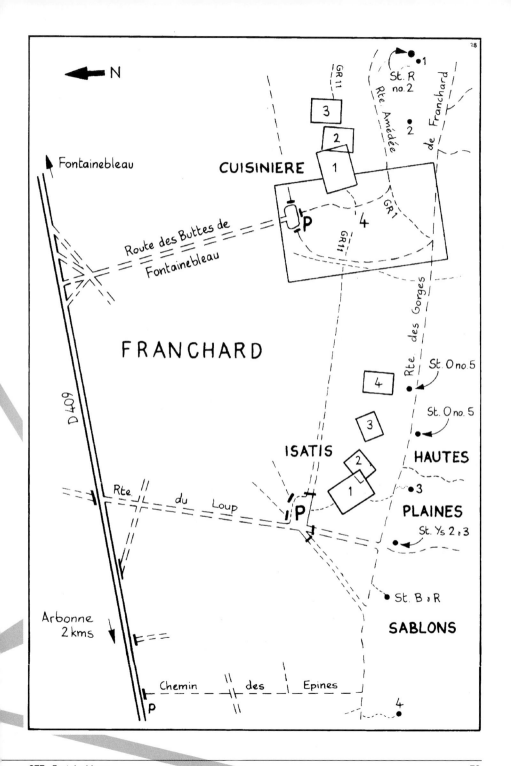

1 **1W 5+ 1b 5+**   START White 6a
Fun L to R traverse in the corridor to the R.
2 2W 4
3 1R 4   START Red
4 3W 4+ 3b 5-
5 10   START Orange
6 2R 4+ Down and L to R
7 3R 4+
8 **4W Le Hareng Saur 5** L of the 4W is 7a+, just to the R, 7c Both'll need a brush.
9 **5W 5+**
10 Old 5R **6a** L to R along rising break New 5R L to R with feet in break. A fair bit easier!
11 **5bW 6c**
12 Rencard 7a
12b 6a/b
13 7R 4+ To the R is **Dimanche Noir 6b**
14 **8R 5-**
15 6c Short steep wall exits L or R
16 30
17 11W 5+
18 9R 5- 9b 4+ round the arete to the R
19 6R 4
20 **6W 6a**
21 7W 4
22 4R 4+
23 **8bW 6a**
24 **8W 5**
25 **20**
26 **9W 5**
27 **10W 6b 10b 6c**
28 180
29 30R 4+   END Red
The R side of arete gives a good problem. Behind is a R to L, Fighting Spirit 6c+
30 **Karma 8a** A long-standing project, this became an instant classic when it was first climbed by Fred Nicole in the autumn of 1995.
31 6a
32 **160**
33 **26R 5**
34 29R 4
35 28R 4+
36 27R 4-

37 170
38 **43W 6b** Dyno to jug from painful crimps 43b 5+ The L hand line **43c 7a t**he excellent R hand line
39 **44W 6b**
40 **Liaison Futile 8a** R to L
41 45W 4+
42 **Eclipse 7b+** R to L Start just L of the tree.
43 **Atomic Power 7b+** The neat wall has painful holds. The R arete can be climbed on its L side – about 7a.

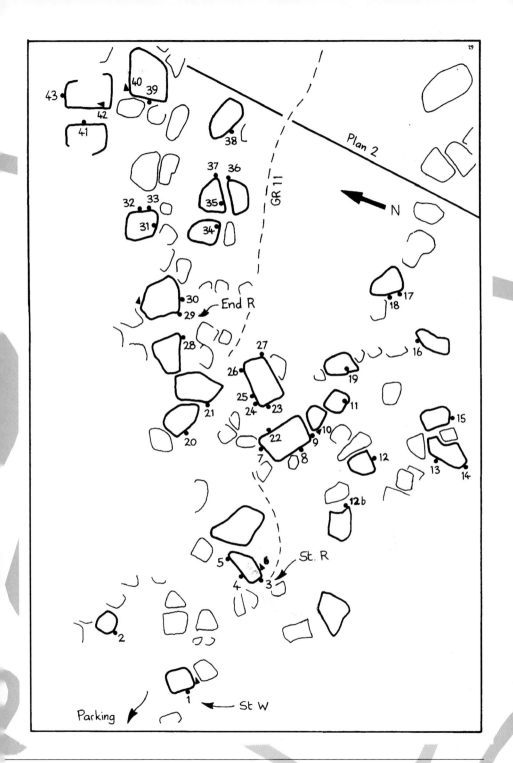

1   10R 4
2   12W 4+ 12b 4
3   11R 4+/5+
4   12R 5-
5   13W 5-
6   13R 4-
7   14W 4+
8   16R 4+
9   **Uranus 7a+** 7c+ with sitting start
10 15R 4-6 Height dependent.
    Just round the R arete, 6b
11 14R 6a
12 50
13 15W 5+
14 23W 5-
15 22W 5-
16 21W 5
16a Haute Tension 7b

16b La Déferlante 7b Big dyno from poor-
    crimps. Spotter essential.
17 17R 5-
18 16W 5
19 18W 4
20 19R 4
21 19W 5+
22 17W 5+
23 18R 4+
24 20W 5+
Corps Accord 7b+ is 4m L.
25 20R 5-
26 22R 4+
27 37W 5
28 7c Bold overhanging wall. Top rope
29 23R 4
30 0
31 39W 5

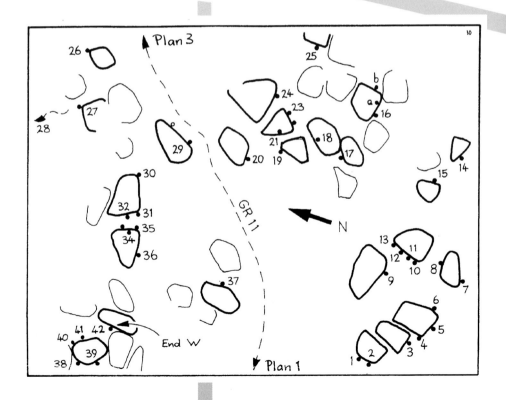

32 **40W 5+**
33 150
34 24R 5
35 41W 5+
36 **42W 5+**
37 25R 4+
38 46W 5+
39 47W 6a
40 **L'Orfevre 6c**
41 **6b**
42 **48W 6b**   END White

Cuisinière plan 3

1 21R 4+
2 120
3 28W 5
4 24W 5+

5 25W 5+
6 26W 5- 26b 5 Just around the R arete is a
    fingery 6c.
7 27W 6a
8 **100**
9 29W 5+ 29b 5-
10 30W 5+ 30b 6a
11 31W 5+
12 32W 4+
13 33W 4
14 **Echine 7b**
15 **L'Innomé** (aka **Le Magnifique**) **7a** Superb
    crimpy wall with slopey finish.
16 **34W 5+**
17 **35W 5+**
18 **36W 6b**

This black circuit has been retraced (very discreetly) to include some superb recent additions. It has some of the best problems for their respective grades in the forest...

The boulders on the map are not to scale.

1 6a
1b 7a+ R to L
2 La Mangouste 6a
3 Excalibur 7a
4 6a
5 Descente aux Enfers 7a+
6 6a
7 Le Merluchet 6c
8 Moondance 6a
9 Blocage Mental 6b
10 Le Pommeau Rédempteur 6a
11 Little Big Gueule 6c
11b 7a R to L
12 La Rastatouille 7a
13 La Charognerie 6c+
14 Rendez Vous à Vautour City 6a
15 Erik le Rouge 6b
16 Le Ketil 6a
17 La Débonnaire 7b
18 La Récréation 7a
19 7a
19b 7a R to L (7b+ without high holds)

Across the two paths from no.19, after about 100m, is a nifty pocket covered roof. You may have to hunt a little...

20 La Cochonnaille 6a
21 Jambon Volant 6b
22 Mosquito Coast 7a Top rope
23 La Mouche 7b+
24 Chimpanzodrome 6c R to L
25 6c+
26 Trois Hommes et un Coup Fin 7b Top rope
27 Gazomètre 6a
Follow the ridge east from here to find the no.2 red circuit, some old black problems, Hale Bopp and Toutes Peines Confondues.
28 Barbatruc 7b
29 La Malbrossé 6a
30 De Fil en Aguille 6b
31 Joli Bouse 6c To the L...**La Chose 7c+**

32 La Châtaigne 7a
33 La Teigne 7a Climbs the L side of the superb prow. Exits direct or swing R. Top is worth a brush.
34 Duel 8a A candidate for the finest hard slab in the forest.

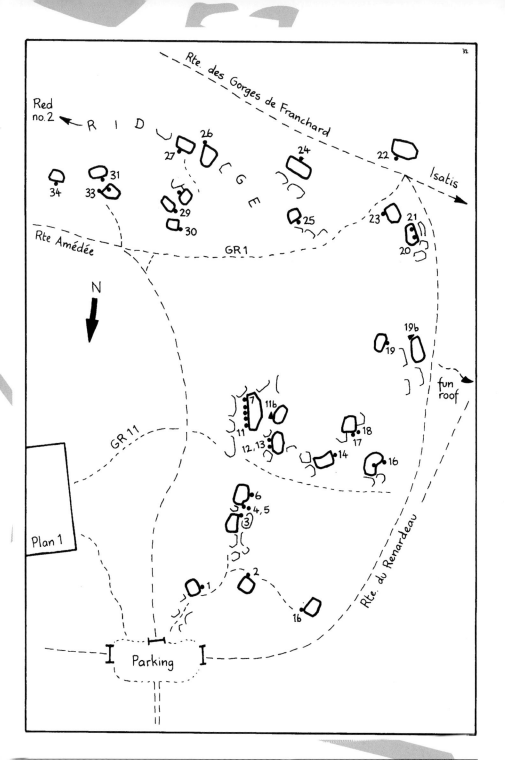

MEGA-GRIP is a liquid that you spread thinly on your hands and when it dries it:
REDUCES SWEAT ON HANDS BY ANT-PERSPIRANT ACTION
USE ON ITS OWN FOR BOULDERING OR AS A BASE ON LONGER CHALK ROUTES
GIVES A AMAZING IMPROVEMENT IN GRIP

It's totally revolutionary, and because of ut's unique formulation MEGA-GRIP doesn't clog up holds like chalk or resin.

MEGA-GRIP does not damage your skin, climbing wall holds or real rock.
WITH MEGA-GRIP HELP TO DECREASE CHALK TRAILS ON ROCK AND BOULDERS AND CLIMB BETTER.

MEGA-GRIP

Respect the Rock
Reduce Dust
and Visual Chalk Pollution
Improve Climbing Performance

Adrenalin **PANTS and TIGHTS**

Made for climbing, mountain biking, walking mountain running. Uses a brilliany new fabric **Tek-Stretch** that dries bloody rapidly, has a two day stretch, breathes, and is amazingly abrasion resistant.

Adrenalin embroidered designs on tees, vests hooded tops, chalk bags.

BALLS TO CHALK
GOOLIES
CHALK BALLS

BLOCK MAGIC
value for money block chalk

Ask your retailer or internet sales via **www.bluedome.co.uk**
Distributed by CAIRN
Tel/Fax +44 (0)145 787 8875   email adrenalin@zen.co.uk

ISATIS

DIRECTIONS

Isatis lies just west of Cuisinière, about 2.5kms east of Arbonne on the D409. Approaching from the west, take the second R turn (the first is normally barred) shortly after the "Forêt Domaniale" sign. This will lead you to the carpark in about 500m.
From the carpark a small path leads to the rocks in about 50m.

CHARACTER

Gets extremely busy at weekends, when queues can form. Like Cuisinière this has a lot of tree cover but dries faster. Plenty of shade in warmer weather.

CLIMBING

Orange no.5 AD (45 problems) A good clearly traced circuit. If you're hungry for more at the end it finishes just across the path from the start of les Hautes Plaines orange.
The next three circuits are very worn but classic. There are plans to repaint them so in the lists I've just noted the colours of the problems and not the numbers.
Blue D- (50 problems)
Red TD (66 problems)
White ED- (55 problems) Varied climbing with a fingery bias. Some bold/high problems although most landings are good.

SABLONS

DIRECTIONS

As for Isatis as far as the carpark. Then follow la Route du Loup until it joins la Route des Gorges de Franchard. Turn right and the problems begin off to the left after about 100m.

CHARACTER

Quieter than neighbouring Isatis and slow to dry.

CLIMBING

Blue D (40 problems)
Red TD (32 problems)

Two good circuits and some excellent recent additions; traverses and straight ups.

HAUTES PLAINES

DIRECTIONS

As for Isatis to the carpark, then Sablons as far as la Route des Gorges de Franchard. The yellows start straight ahead and off to the L. For the orange turn L and follow la Route des Gorges de Franchard for about 400m. The start is off to the R.

CHARACTER

Slow drying and very quiet.

CLIMBING

Yellow no.2 PD- (44 problems)
Yellow PD+ (25 problems)
Orange no.5 AD+ (43 problems)

1 W 4+   START White
2 **Wb L'Amoche Doigt 6b**
3 **Surprise 7b+** The central weakness is slightly easier with crafty L toe hook. Sit down start **7c/7c+**? Mystification 8b L to R Start L of 3 to exit up 2. Utterly desperate!
4 **7a** L and R versions.
5 W 5
6 B 3+
7 B 4
8 W 5
9 **R 5**
10 **W 5**
11 **R 5 L'Intégrale 7b+** L to R From 11 to18
12 W 5
13 R 5-
14 R 4+
15 **W 5**
16 **W Composition des Forces 6c**
Just R Couanne de Merde 7a+
17 R 4
18 B 3-
19 W 6a
20 **R 4+**
21 R 5
22 B 3+
23 W 7a
24 **Super Joker 7c**
25 **W Le Coup de Pompe 5+** Exit direct or just R
26 **W Le Statique 5+** Pure thuggery
27 W 5
28 R 4
29 B 3+
30 W 6a
31 To the L Rick Hochet 7a To the R 7a both bold.
32 **R 5** R to L exit up weakness in corridor. **Lamentations 7c** L to R: Start at 32 exit up 34. **Pierres en Pleurs 8a+** L to R: Start at 32 exit up 35.
And three fingery, bold classics all guaranteed to give a very big buzz...
33 **Gymnopédie 7c** Rising Rward line with same finish as...

34 **Le Mur des Lamentations 7b+** Arguably the finest climb at the grade in the forest. Aka the 12bis.
35 **Gnossiène 7c** Rising Lward line. Finish just R of 12 bis.
36 B 3+
37 B 2+ L to R
38 R 5 Just to the L Les Boules 6c
39 **R 5- 7a+** R to L from 39 to finish up 41
40 R 5
41 **W Envie des Bêtes 6b** Either out R from slimey undercuts, up, then back diagonally L, or straight up and R via obvious crimp to join above. Direct up the 'crack' is **6c+**
42 **W Le Balancier 5-** Possible static or with an ungradeable double-dyno.
43 R 5-
44 **W La Zip Zut 6b** Easier with boss.
45 **B 5-**
46 R 4
   6a R to L Start R of 46 exit up L arete
47 L to R?
48 R 4+
49 W Le Vin Blanc 5 goes up and R
Just R **Le Vin Aigre 7c+/8a** leaps direct from nasty crimp.
50 R 5
51 R 4
52 W 5
53 R 4+
54 **Beurre Marga 6a+** Lovely, finger friendly exercise in the use of rounded sidepulls. Rising L to R. R hand line to same finishing hold is also good but a little harder.

From here you can take the small path and try **le Surplomb de la Coquille 6c+** (see Franchard map).

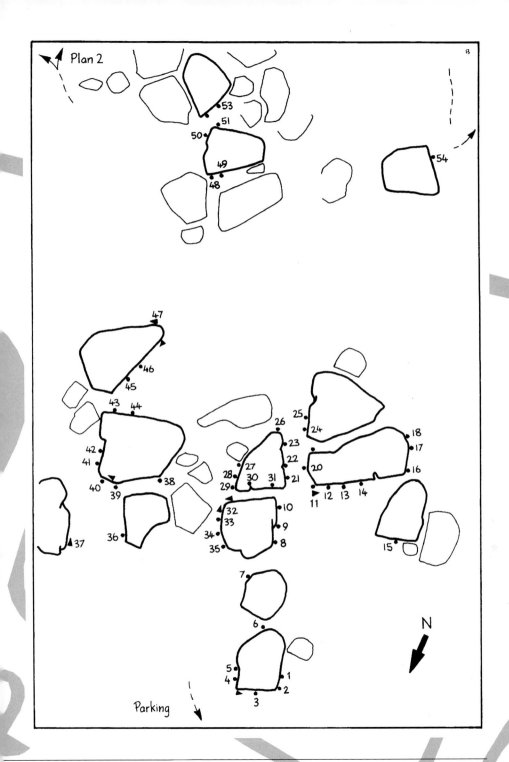

Plan 2

N

Parking

1 B 4
2 W La Planquée 6b
3 W 6a
4 W 5+
5 B 4 L to R
6 B 3
7 W 4+
8 R 5+
9 R 5+
10 B 4
11 W 6a
12 W 5+
13 R 5+ R to L and up
14 R 4
15 B 3+
16 R 4+
17 R 4
18 R 5 Rising R ward traverse
19 W La Farine 6a
20 R 4+
21 B 4-
22 R 5- direct B 4 L to R

23 W 5+
24 W 6a R to L
25 B 4-
26 6b Up and R Bold
27 B 3+
28 4-
29 B 2
30 B 3+
31 W 6b

Isatis Plan 3
1 R 5
2 B 4
3 R 5
4 W 4+
5 R left, 3 right 6a
6 330 2
7 320 2
8 W 6a (without arete)
9 W 6a Direct is 6b

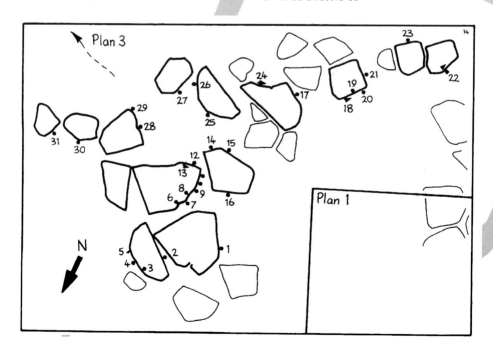

10 W 5
11 R 4
12 W 5
13 W 6a
14 B 4
15 W 6b Left side of arete. Angle Ben's 7a+ Right side
16 B 3
17 bO 3+
18 340 1+
19 W 6a
20 W 6a
21 W 5+
22 R 5
23 W 5+
24 R 5
25 B 3
26 360 2+
27 L to R 5+
28 6a Direct from back of roof. **Le Faux Baquet 7a** Finish R wards via pocket (the

"false jug") without arete.
29 W 6b Roof+crack reaching up and R.
Wb 6a+ R to L under roof and up 28
30 B 4+/5
31 R 4
32 Enigma 7b+/8b? High pain tolerance essential. Eliminate the obvious low foothold to the L and it's much harder – and unrepeated.
33 Alta 7c+ Powerful undercut start to tricky finish.
34 370 2+

Not on the plan 80m east is a classic problem which climbs the undercut nose of a huge boulder, **El Poussah 6c/7a** The poor man's La Bérézina. Short but sweet. The key is to use a weird toe hook high on the R. In good conditions thugs can eliminate this frustrating (until you get the knack) manoeuvre by yarding up the slopers footless. 7b from low on the R.

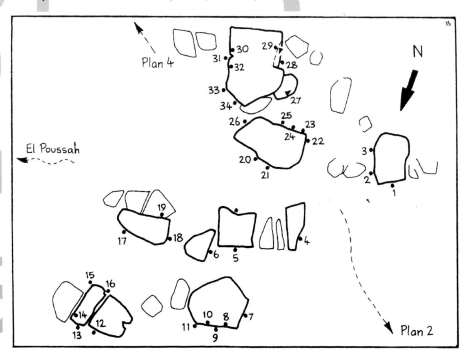

1 B 3
2 B 4-
3 R 5
4 R 4
5 W 5 L to R and up
6 R 4 Ape L along lip and mantel whenever it takes your fancy.
7 W Le Memel 7b
8 R 4+
9 B 3+
10 Ob 2+
11 Project?
12 R 4+
13 0 2
14 B 3
15 W 6c direct   6b with arete
                              END White
16 W La Patinoire 5
17 W 6a L to R and up
18 W 6c
19 R La Bissouflante 5
20 R 5
21 B 4-

22 90 3
23 R 5
24 W 6b L to R and up. The last, straight up bit is a good 5+ in its own right
25 L'Arrache Coeur 7c Impressive, high and neglected. First climbed by Anthoine le Menestrel in 1983.

Explorers can continue the red circuit which follows the ridge eastwards, finishing not far from Cuisinière.

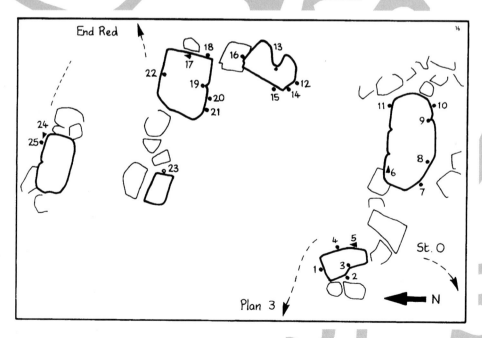

PREPARATION IS THE KEY TO SUCCESS.
HE IS, ARE YOU?

BOLT ON HOLDS, FINGER BOARDS, CAMPUS BOARDS, ACCESSORIES

S7
TRAINING
ESSENTIALS

BEN MOON ON KARMA, 8A

TEL/FAX: 0114 221 9356

DIRECTIONS

Les Gorges du Houx

Take the D301 circular road and park at a small parking space on a bend between le Carrefour de la Croix de Franchard and le Carrefour des Gorges de Franchard. Follow the Route du Mont Aigu east, heading down a little valley, for about 400m. The start of the circuit is just L of the path.

Mont Aigu

As the N7 goes into Fontainebleau from the NW it goes down a hill to a big set of lights. From here take the D409 direction Milly then the first turn on the L. Follow this trending L to arrive at a carpark after about 600m. Take the Route du Levraut until the Carrefour de l'Emérillon. Then the Route des Gorges de Franchard eastwards for about 300m. Turn R where the sentier blue crosses the path. The circuits begin here.

Franchard East

Take the D301 circular road and park at the Carrefour des Gorges de Franchard. Walk west along the Route des Gorges de Franchard for about 1km. The starts off the circuits are off to the R, the black just after a R turn, the red just before it.

CHARACTER

Les Gorges du Houx Very quiet and quick drying.

Mont Aigu Beautiful spot. Shady at the bottom. More open at the top. Dries fairly fast.

Franchard East Very quiet and slow drying.

CLIMBING

Les Gorges du Houx

Yellow PD- (21 problems) Beginner's circuit.

Mont Aigu

Yellow PD (25 problems)
Orange AD (48 problems)
Blue D+/TD- (56 problems)
The orange and blue are both very fine, finishing on the same bloc up on the ridge. Some high problems and/or bad landings.

Franchard East

Red D+/TD-
Black TD+ (123 problems) Nature has taken over much of this ancient and virtually abandoned circuit. Some impressive problems that are hardly ever climbed.

And for strong trainspotters...

1 **Petit Tome 7b** Excellent L to R traverse. Queues unlikely. Park at the Carrefour de l'Occident, 1.25km south of le Carrefour des Gorges de Franchard. Take the track going east and turn R onto a path that goes L down a small valley. It's up on the small escarpment R (south) of the path.

2 **Inaccessible Absolu 7c** Aptly named. Climbs the very impressive steep wall overlooking the path. Unrepeated and totally neglected. Worked on a rope but soloed afterwards. As for les Gorges de Houx yellow. Then continue on the same path until le Carrefour de Franchière. The bloc is up to the L (NW of the carrefour). 15 minutes from carpark.

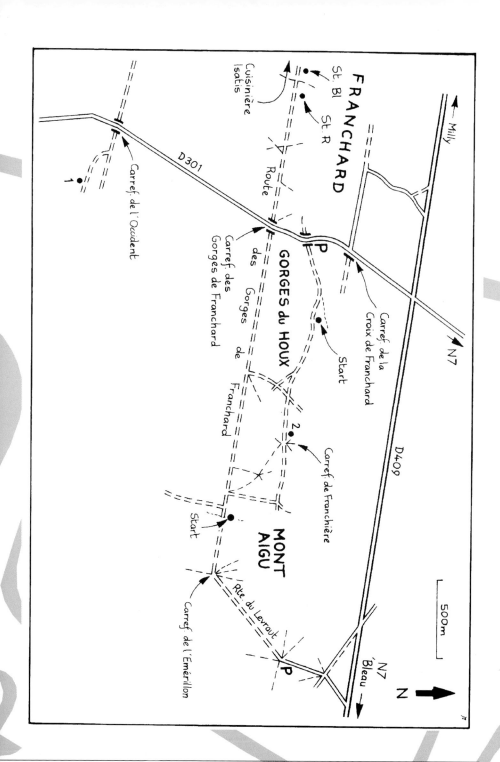

DIRECTIONS

Situated just south of Fontainebleau, off the N6 a little over 2kms east of the Carrefour de l'Obélisque. You may have to try once or twice before finding the right layby to park in. Walk into the woods, cross the Carrefour de Mayenne and head up the slope, soon taking a smaller path up and left to find the start of the orange circuit and the hard problems.

CHARACTER

Quiet and slow drying.

CLIMBING

Orange AD- (20 problems) Old and worn but some good problems.

Plus three worthwhile hard problems on la Dame Jeanne, the large boulder just L of the orange start:

Calamity Jeanne 7b climbs the weakness in the impressive wall.

Cosa Nostra 7c starts up Calamity Jeanne, then traverses diagonally R to finish up the left-slanting crack. Complex, bold climbing.

On the other side of this bloc is a brilliant **7a** crack. There is potential for more new problems here.

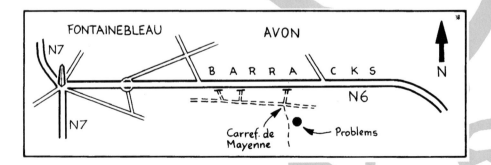

DIRECTIONS

About 2kms south of Fontainebleau. From the Carrefour de l'Obélisque take the N152 for 2.5 kms and park at the end of le champ de manoeuvres. Follow the edge of the champ to find a path which takes you to le Carrefour de la Plaine de Mont Morillon. The circuit starts close to the SE corner of the carrefour.

CHARACTER

Extremely quiet and slow drying.

CLIMBING

Orange AD- (26 problems) A grubby start leads to a fine finish on the more exposed ridge.

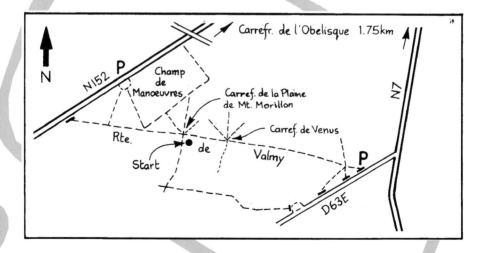

DIRECTIONS
Situated off la Route de la Plaine de la Haute Borne which cuts a more or less straight line between the D301 to the east and the D64 to the west (which runs north/south between Arbonne and Achères, beside the A6). Park at the Carrefour de la Haute Borne and follow the GR1 south-east for about 500m, trending slightly left at the crossroads. Shortly after the crossroads take a small path which cuts off to the right and follow it until it meets another, much bigger path. Follow this to the right for about 75m and the rocks are obvious just off to your right.

CHARACTER
So quiet it's almost frightening! The rocks get plenty of sun and dry fast. Probably too hot in summer at least for the harder problems.

CLIMBING
A strange, extremely esoteric little massif. There's nothing wrong with the easier problems but most of those who take the trouble to come here will have their eyes on In Extremis and a few of the other difficult problems, which are hard on the fingers and technical. Because most of the climbs are in narrow corridors, falling off can be dodgy so come with a good spotter. In Extremis may or may not have a top roping bolt at its top.

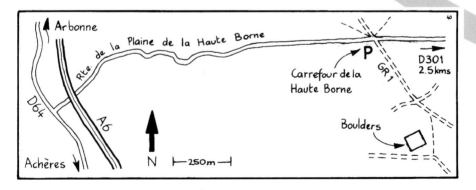

1 5-
2 7a
3 6a
4 Etat d'Ivresse 5
5 4+
6 5+
7 5-
8 6a
9 No Man's Land 6c
10 In Extremis 7b
10b L'Excuse 7a
11 Le Maître des Lieux 7a
12 4-
13 6b
14 5+
15 5
16 6b
17 5
18 5-
19 4-

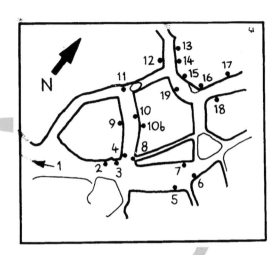

THE EDGE CLIMBING CENTRE

**New and Extensive Bouldering
Air Conditioning
Quality Climbs
Moving Walls**

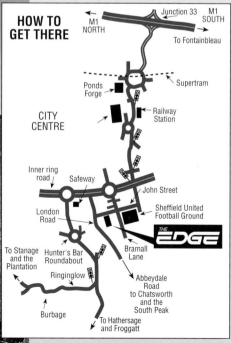

HOW TO GET THERE

Junction 33 M1 SOUTH
M1 NORTH
To Fontainbleau
Supertram
Ponds Forge
CITY CENTRE
Railway Station
Inner ring road
Safeway
John Street
London Road
Sheffield United Football Ground
THE EDGE
To Stanage and the Plantation
Hunter's Bar Roundabout
Bramall Lane
Ringinglow
Abbeydale Road to Chatsworth and the South Peak
Burbage
To Hathersage and Froggatt

THE EDGE CLIMBING CENTRE
John Street, Bramall Lane, Sheffield, S2 4QU
☎ 0114 2758899

Photo by Dave Simmonite

OPEN 7 DAYS A WEEK

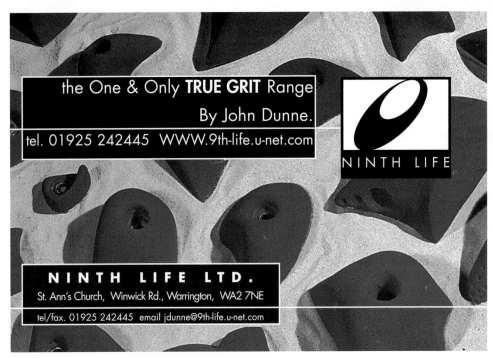

the One & Only **TRUE GRIT** Range
By John Dunne.
tel. 01925 242445   WWW.9th-life.u-net.com

NINTH LIFE

NINTH LIFE LTD.
St. Ann's Church, Winwick Rd., Warrington, WA2 7NE

tel/fax. 01925 242445   email jdunne@9th-life.u-net.com

ROCK ON

BULGING WITH
CLIMBING GEAR

Many shops claim to be
climbing specialists.
At **Rock On** we sell
Climbing / Mountaineering
equipment & books and
absolutely nothing else.
NOTHING ELSE
Now that's specialist!!

Rock On
at YHA Adventure Shops
14 Southampton Street
Covent Garden, London WC2E 7HY
Tel: 0171 836 8541

Rock On
at
Birmingham Climbing Centre
A.B.Row
Birmingham B4 7RB
Tel: 0121 359 8709

DIRECTIONS

From le Carrefour de l'Obélisque follow the D58, direction Bourron-Marlotte. After 6km, just before entering the village by la Maison Forestière, turn left (east) onto a track and follow this, trending left, to its end and a carpark. The easiest access for the red circuit is to follow la Route de la Plaine Verte eastward for about 150m before turning right onto the sentier bleu. This eventually weaves its way round to the start of the circuit.

For the orange either follow la Route de la Mort north and turn right along la Route du Long Rocher or shorter take la Route de Languedoc which slogs up the hill onto the plateau to bring you out at la Grotte Béatrix, just above the end of the orange circuit. Below the cave the sentier bleu will take you round to the start of the circuit.

CHARACTER

It doesn't get much quieter than this! A magical spot where you may simply prefer to sit cross legged on a rock and meditate. It dries slowly and due to its (totally undeserved) unpopularity and deep forest setting, the tops of some problems may need a brush.

CLIMBING

Orange AD- (33 problems) Traditional mountaineering circuit with some fine boulders.

Red TD (33 problems) One of the forest's best kept secrets. Fingery, strenuous climbing in general, a few nasty landings but constant interest.

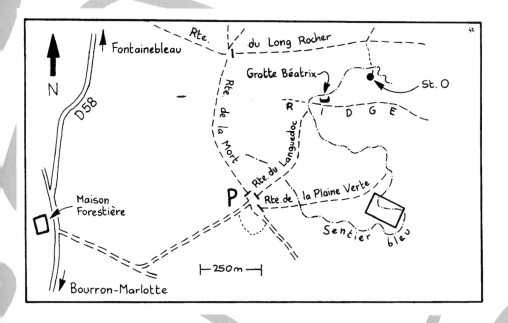

The red circuit:

1 5-
2 **Le Portique 5**
3 **Elixir de Bouldering 6a L to R**
3b **5**
4 4
5 5-
5b **Destroy Men 6a**
6 5
7 5-
8 4
9 5
10 5
11 4
12 5-
13 4
14 4
15 Les Lames 4+
16 5+
17 5
18 4
19 4-
20 5
21 Hyper Gratton 5-
22 **Le Pascalien 5**
23 **L'Impossible 6a**
24 4+
25 4
26 **La Tendinite 6a**
27 **Ballade sous les Toits 5** Rising L to R and up via hole.
28 4+
29 5-
30 4
31 5+
32 4
33 5-
34 5

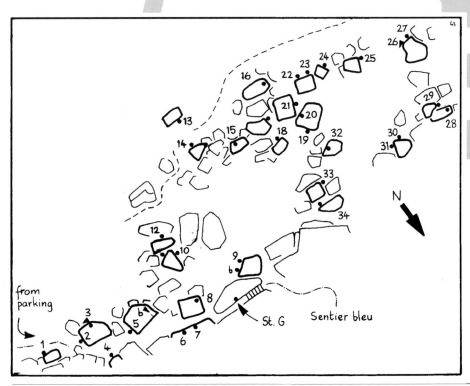

BENDCRETE
CLIMBING WALLS

Bolt-on holds and training aids to design and installation of all styles of climbing structures including articulated walls.

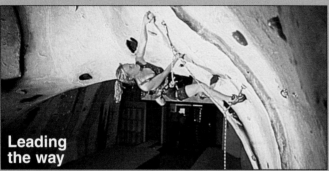

Leading the way

Ruth Jenkins in action on the Plas y Brenin Climbing Wall built by Bendcrete

For more information on our quality products contact:

BENDCRETE
CLIMBING WALLS

Aqueduct Mill, Tame Street, Stalybridge, Cheshire SK15 1ST
Tel: 0161 338 3046 Fax: 0161 338 7956

WORN OUT?

Fontainbleau circuits are as demanding on your footwear as they are on your body.

The problem with today's performance rock boots is that by the time you've softened them up enough to be wearable, they're practically worn out!

WORN IN...

Feet First specialise in resoling worn out rock boots. This is of special benefit to the boulderer who really appreciates a pair of well worn-in boots - softened for maximum comfort and resoled in one of a choice of the stickiest rubbers on the market.

Go on ... treat your feet to a pair of old boots.

CALL OR WRITE FOR A **FREE** COLOUR BROCHURE

Factory
Units 4-5, Foundry Street Ind. Estate,
Whittington Moor, Chesterfield S41 9AU
Tel: (01246) 260795

Shop
728 Chesterfield Road,
Woodseats, Sheffield S8 0SE
Tel: (0114) 258 9529

feet**first** - specialist outdoor footwear resolers

Aurore Brun enjoying the solitude on a grade 4 at Les Gorge aus Chats. Jacky Godoffe

Even at areas famous for their difficult problems there are hundreds of more amenable grades. And Cuvier is no exception...Niall Grimes

TROIS PIGNONS

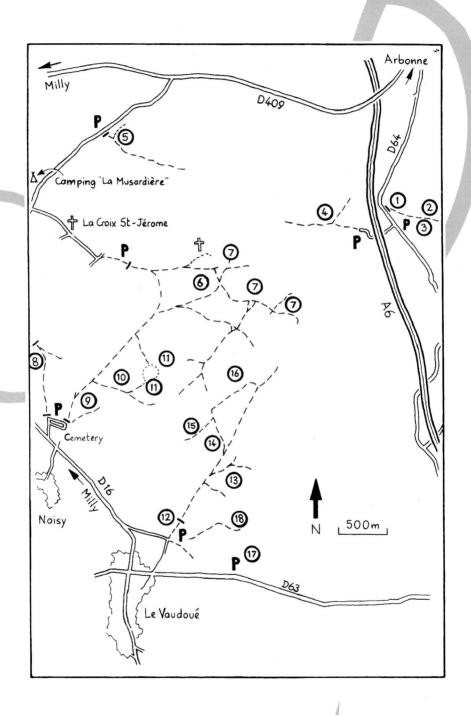

Milly

D409

Arbonne

D64

A6

P

⑤

△ Camping "La Musardière"

✝ La Croix St-Jérome

P

✝

⑦

⑥

⑦

⑦

④

P

①

②

P

③

⑧

⑪

⑩

⑪

⑯

P

⑨

Cemetery

⑮

⑭

D16

Milly

Noisy

⑬

N

500m

⑫

P

⑱

P ⑰

D63

Le Vaudoué

Left: The evergreen Jo Montchaussé on the 22R 5+, La Roche aux Sabots. Jacky Godoffe **Above: Le Cul de Chien in autumn.** Steve Gough **Below: Josh Rimmer tearing up the children's circuit at Beauvais.** Neil Pearsons

FAX09 - PEAK BOULDERING

by Allen Williams and Alan James

All the best bouldering in the Peak District in one book

3D topos, symbols, maps and tick lists

Everything you have come to expect from;

ROCK FAX

AVAILABLE NOVEMBER 1997

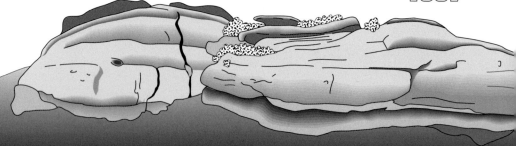

The Secret Garden   VERTICAL BRAIN ☎ 0114 2507760

DIRECTIONS

From Arbonne take the D64 heading south. After about 2kms the road bends to the L, within spitting distance of the A6. After the bend park at either one of 2 carparks on the L.

For the boulders follow the Chemin du Bois Rond eastwards (from the 2nd carpark a path cuts through the woods to meet it) for about 500m. The start of the circuits are clearly visible on either side of the path.

CHARACTER

Le Rocher de la Reine

South facing, this is open and quick drying for the most part. Up on the ridge there are superb views in all directions. Never busy.

Le Bois Rond

Lower and less exposed but still dries fast. It's rare to see foreign visitors here but it's popular with the locals.

Drei Zinnen

Quiet and fairly quick drying.

CLIMBING

Rocher de la Reine

Yellow PD+ (48 problems) Long and varied. Excellent for beginners.

Blue D+ (57 problems) Another good varied circuit. Some tricky and at times bold problems.

Le Bois Rond

Orange AD (37 problems)

Blue D+ (33 problems)

Red ED- (40 problems)

Three excellent, varied circuits, all providing a good test at their respective levels. The red circuit is very fingery and can become horribly difficult in Summer. Landings are generally good.

Drei Zinnen

Blue D (39 problems)

There are plans for a red circuit. There are some hefty boulders here, both on and off circuit. A jumble of boulders up on the ridge, behind the water authority building, are particularly impressive with some futuristic lines.

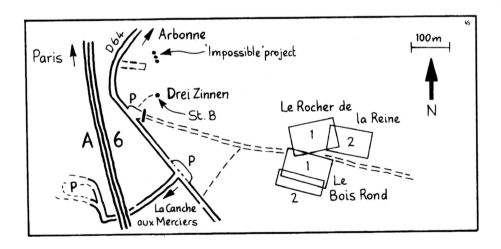

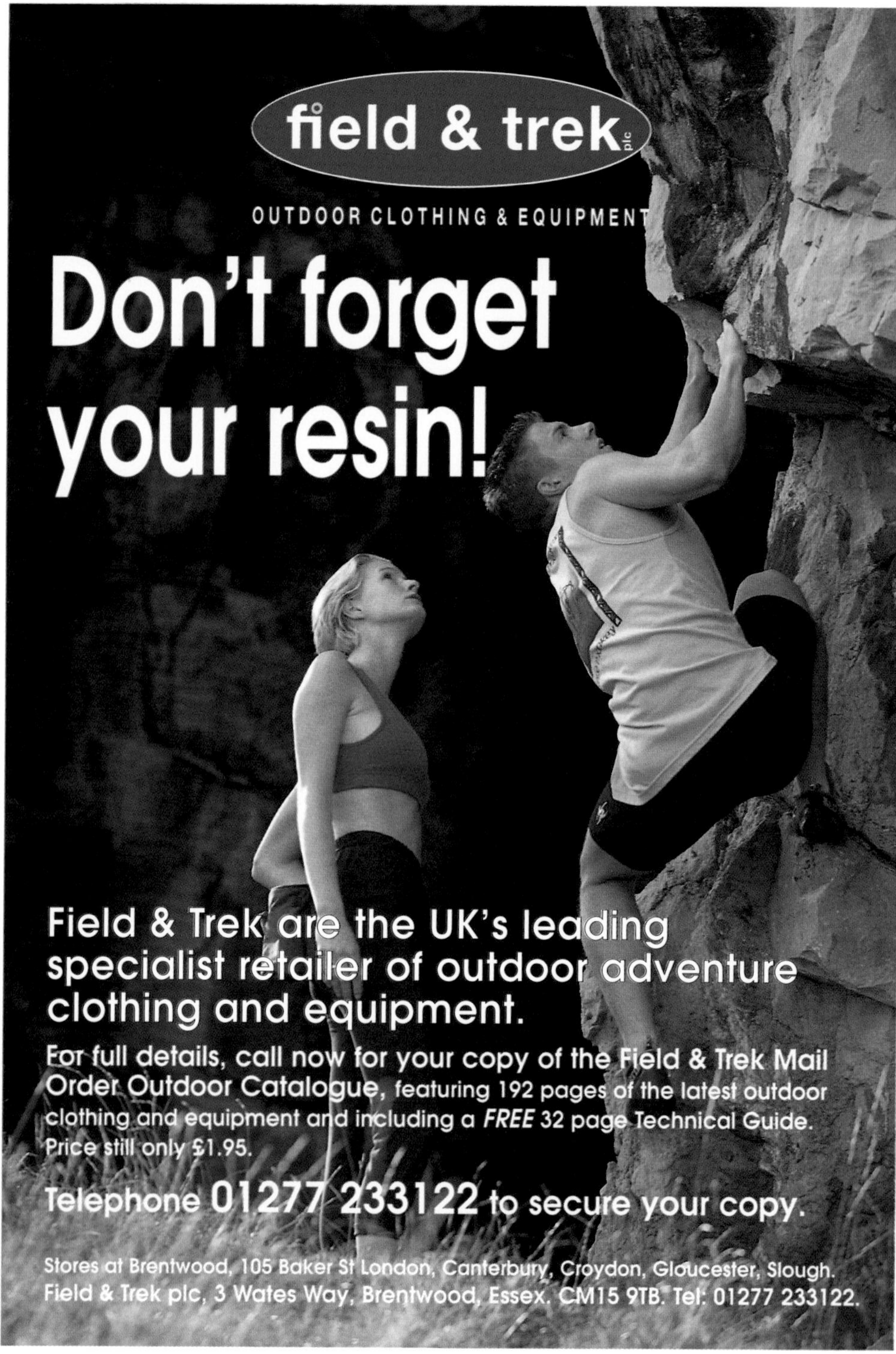
field & trek plc
OUTDOOR CLOTHING & EQUIPMENT
Don't forget your resin!
Field & Trek are the UK's leading specialist retailer of outdoor adventure clothing and equipment.
For full details, call now for your copy of the Field & Trek Mail Order Outdoor Catalogue, featuring 192 pages of the latest outdoor clothing and equipment and including a FREE 32 page Technical Guide. Price still only £1.95.
Telephone 01277 233122 to secure your copy.
Stores at Brentwood, 105 Baker St London, Canterbury, Croydon, Gloucester, Slough.
Field & Trek plc, 3 Wates Way, Brentwood, Essex. CM15 9TB. Tel: 01277 233122.

Above Michel Libert, the man who first climbed L'Abbatoir, on Les Frites 7R 5+, Cuvier Jacky Godoffe
Below: Sociable bouldering at Rocher Fin. Stéphan Denys

1	1Y 2	START Yellow
2	2Y 2	
3	3Y 2	
4	4Y 2	
5	5Y 3	
6	6Y 2	
7	7Y 2	
8	8Y 2	
9	9Y 2	
10	10Y 2	
11	1B 5-	START Blue
12	2B 4-	
13	3B 4-	
14	4B 4	
15	5B 4-	
16	6B 3+	
17	7B 4-	
18	8B 4	
19	13Y 2	
20	11Y 2	
21	12Y 3	
22	9B 5-	
23	10B 4 R to L	
24	56Y	
25	11B 4-	
26	12B 3+	
27	21B 4 21b 5+	
28	52Y	
29	58Y	END Yellow
30	20B 5-	
31	18B 4	
32	19B 3	
33	17B 4	
34	16B 3-	
35	15B 4-	
36	14B 3+	
37	13B 4+	
38	22B 4-	
39	48Y	
40	29B 4	
41	15Y	
42	18Y	
43	25B 4-	
44	24B 4- 24b 4+	
45	16Y	
46	26B 5+ 26b 4-	

47	19Y
48	20Y
49	29B 4
50	30B 4
51	27B 4+
52	31B 3
53	32B 3
54	46Y
55	47Y

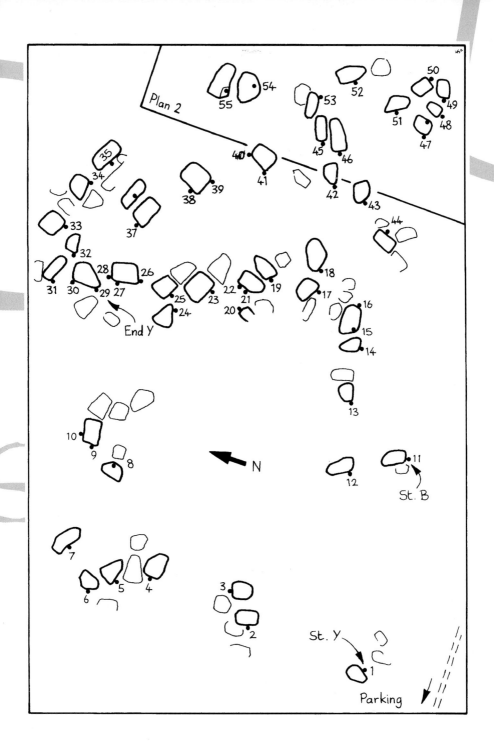

Plan 2

End Y

N

St. B

St. Y

Parking

Benoit Faure on Le Pendule de Foucault 8b, Cuvier. Left: Olivier and friends at le Rocher du Potala. Both Stéphan Denys

1	33B 5	
2	34B 4+	
3	38Y	
4	44Y	
5	42B 4	
6	43Y	
7	43B 4	
8	42Y	
9	44B 4+	
10	40Y	
11	39Y	
12	41B 4+	41b 5
13	35B 4-	
14	37Y	
15	36B 4	
16	36Y	
17	37B 4	
18	22Y	
19	23Y	
20	38B 4+	38b 5
21	39B 4-	
22	24Y	
23	25Y	
24	56B 5-	
25	46B 4-	
26	47bB 4	
27	47B 3+	
28	34Y	
29	48B 4+	
30	49B 4	
31	50B 5-	
32	33Y	
33	32Y	
34	31Y	
35	51B 4+	
36	29Y	
37	55B 4+	
38	28Y	
39	27Y	
40	54B 5-	
41	53B 4-	
42	52B 3	52b 4
43	57B	END Blue

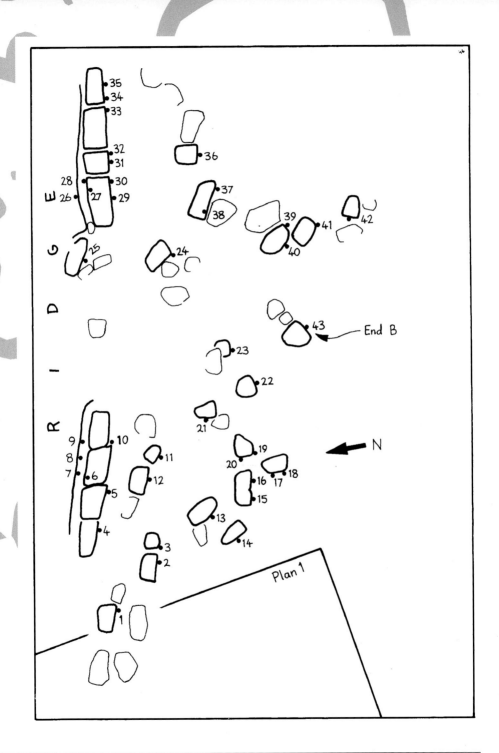

Plan 1

End B

Dany Riche on La Bérézina 7c, Cuvier.
Jacky Godoffé

Eric Gherson on the Mur de la Fosse aux Ours 7a, 95.2. Jo Montchaussé

1	**1R 5**	START Red
2	**2R 6a**	
3	310	
4	**3R 6a** L to R	
5	**28B 5**	
6	320	
7	29B 4	
8	340	
9	**4R 6b**	
10	**5R Kasimodo 6c**	
11	6bR Toubib or not Toubib 5/5+	
12	6R Silver Lago 6a	
13	**7R Little Shakespeare 6a**	
14	**8R Hamlet 5**	
15	30B 5-	
16	**350**	
17	32B 4-	
18	**9R Friction et Réalité 6a**	
19	33B 5	END Blue
20	370	END Orange
21	**10R Objectif Grand Angle 5+**	
22	**Lucky Luke 7c** Just R of LL is Sensation 7b/7b+?	
23	11R Planète Morphos 6a	
24	31B 5	
25	**1B 4**	START Blue
26		START Orange
27	1B 5	
28	10	
29	**20**	
30	**2B 5+**	
31	**12R Haute Calorie 6a/b** L to R	
32	30	
33	**3B 4+**	
34	**13R Glasnost 5+**	
35	**14R Regard de Statue 6b**	
36	50	
37	4B 4	
38	60	
39	**15R L'Amie Dalle 5+**	
40	5B 4	
41	**15tR Morphotype 6c** L to R	
42	70	
43	**6B 4+**	
44	**16R L'Attraction des Pôles 5+**	
45	20B 4	

46	31R 5	
47	21B 4+	
48	260	
49	240	
50	**32R 6c** R to L	
51	270	
52	230	
53	**22B 4**	
54	**33R L'OTAN emporte l'Auvent 5+/6a**	
55	**34R Galla Lactique 6c (7a+** with continuation) L to R	
56	**35R Constellation des Amoureux 6c**	
57	36R 5	
58	**37R Le Long Fleuve Tranquille 5+/6a** L to R	
59	23B 4	
60	290	
61	**38R Le Vélo de Max 6b/c** R to L	
62	39R L'Appui acide 5+ **39b Le T.A. 5/5+**	
63	24B 5	
64	25B 5	
65	40R 5	
66	26B 4+	
67	**Fritz l'Angle 5+**	END Red
68	**300**	

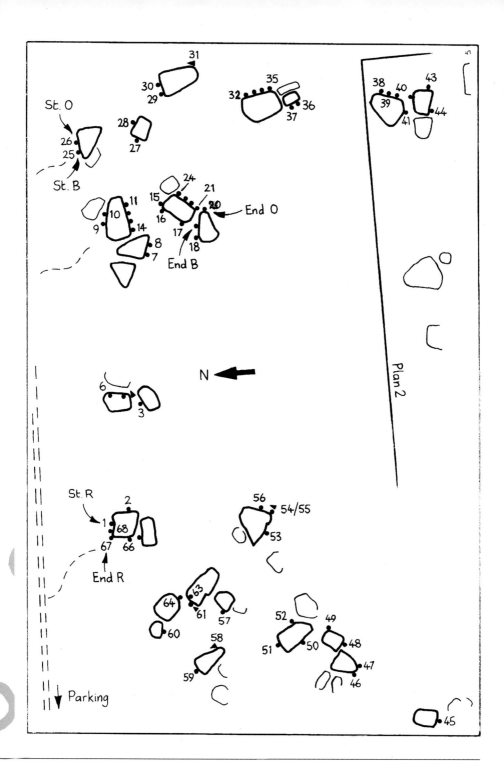

Left: Christophe Bougon attempting L'Angle Parfait 7a+, La Dame Jouanne. Steve Gough
Above: Sybille van den Hove on A L'Impossible... 7a at La Roche aux Sabots. Stéphan Denys
Below: October morning at Cuvier. Steve Gough

1   7B 4+
2   17R 5+
3   80
4   8B 4
5   **5+** Harder without heel hook on arete.
6   18R 6c L to R
7   9B 5-
8   **19R Prise de Becquet 6a**
9   **20R Ponction Lombaire 6a**
10 90
11 100
12 10B 4+
13 11B 4
14 21R 5
15 170
16 160
17 **21bR Tour du Bloc 7a** The whole bloc, L to R. Superb and varied, with the crux near the end.
18 150
19 12B 4+
20 140
21 15B 4
22 **22R Le Meilleur des Mondes 6a** Excellent problem with toe hook the key. Harder for the short.
23 **23R La Théorie des Nuages 6a/b** R to L
24 16B 4+
25 190
26 14B 4+
27 25R 6a   25b6c
28 24R 5+
29 **26R Razorback 5** L to R To the R: **26b 6b** R to L (or **7b** with low exit).
30 13B 4+
31 180
32 28R 5+
33 17B 5-
34 27R Gilette pare Dalle 6a
35 **29R Aero Beuark 6c** R to L
36 19B 5-   19b 4
37 18B
38 **30R Super Vista 6b** L to R   30b 5+

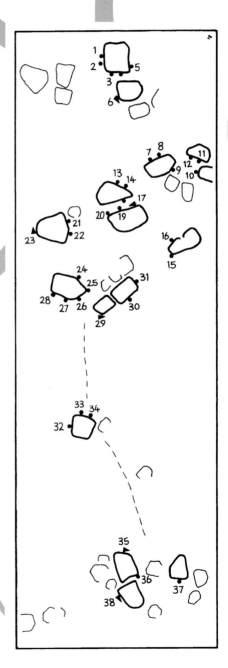

DIRECTIONS

As for le Rocher de la Reine and le Bois Rond, but turn R (coming from Arbonne) opposite the 2nd carpark, signposted la Canche aux Merciers. Parking after 300m.

For the boulders either follow the broad track westward for about 150m before turning R to find the start of plan 1. Alternatively cut through to the path which passes in front of the two derelict houses. The first of the off-circuit traverses listed below is about 100m W of the L hand house.

CHARACTER

Like its neighbours the noise from the A6 detracts from the enjoyment this massif has to offer. There can also be millions of bemused looking soldiers to contend with. It remains however extremely popular, thanks to the ease of access, the wide range of difficulty avaialble, good landings and an open, quick drying aspect.

Look out for VIPERS!

CLIMBING

White (chidren's 33 problems)
Yellow PD- (41 problems)
Orange AD (41 problems)
Blue no. 1 D+ (45 problems)
Red TD+ (33 problems)

Near the derelict houses are several superb unmarked traverses. See map.

1 Ni Vieux ni Bête 7a+ R to L
2 Soléa 7c L to R
3 La Colonne Durruti 7c+ Traverse R, down crack, R, up crack, R to finish. As a variation (8b) you can add a loop by traversing high back L after 2nd crack into 1st crack.

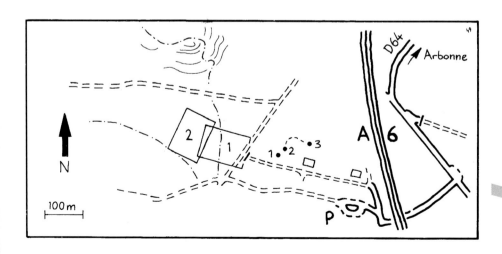

Jacky Godoffe, past and present master of the forest. Left: As a young man climbing La Digitale 5a, Cuvier. Jo Montchaussé Right: In more recent times on Duroxmanie 6c, Cuvier Rempart. Aurore Brun

1	1R 5-	START Red
2	2R 5+ L to R	
3	41Y	
4	10	
5		START Orange
6	3R 5+	
7	1B 4+	START Blue
8	6R 5+	
9	20	
10	2B 4+	
11	5R 5+ 1m L Infusion du Soir 7a	
12	3B 4	
13	39Y	
14	30	
15	4B 4+	
16	38Y	
17	5B 4-	
18	70	
19	7R 5+	
20	80	
21	8B 5- 8b 5	
22	8R 5+	
23	6B 4-	
24	7B 4+	
25	90	
26	100	
27	9B 4-	
28	110	
29	120	
30	11B	
31	17B 5-	
32	10B 4	
33	130	
34	9R 5	
35	19B 5	
36	10R 6a	
37	18B 4-	
38	160	
39	150	
40	140	
41	**16B 4+** 16b 4	
42	15B 4+	
43	33R 5	END Red
44	40B 3+	
45	**32R 6b** R to L	
46	**14B 4**	

47	12B 4- 12b 4-	
48	8Y	
49	13B 3+	
50	30R 5	
51	31R 5+	
52	29R 6a 29b 6c	
53	41B 4	
54	42B 4 R to L	
55	24R 5 L to R	
56	36B 3 36b 4	
57	23R 5-	
58	23R 5	
59	43B 4	
60	27R 6a	
61	**400**	
62	410	END Orange
63	44B 3+	
64	**25R 5+** L to R	
65	**26R 5+**	
66	**45B 5-** 45b 4 END Blue	
67	44Y	END Yellow
On same boulder		START Yellow
68	43Y	

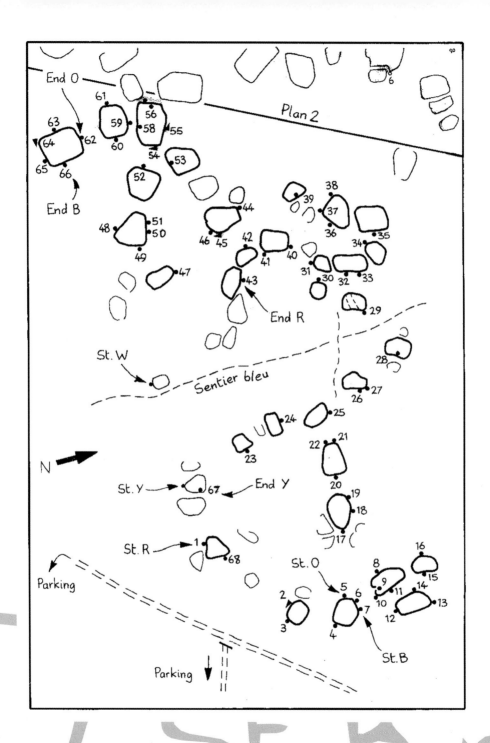

Stéphan Denys employing the cunning
toe-hook on El Poussah 6c/7a, Isatis.
Steve Gough
**Left: Stuart Littlefair flashing Alta
7c/7c+, Isatis.** Stéphan Denys

1   20B 4-
2   190
3   21B 3+
4   200
5   11R 6a
5b   Rage dedans 7b+
6   22B 4   22bB 4 is further R.
    Jacadi 8a is a sitting start dyno to the top,
    L of crack of 22bB and R of...
7   12R 6b
Also here; **La Longue Marche 7c** Start low and
trav R along horizontal crack. Up blue bis and
back L along lip until holds run out.
8   13R 6a L to R
9   14R 6a
10   230
11   250
12   15R 5+
13   7b R to L traverse. Exit opposite 12.
14   260
15   7a+ R to L traverse.
16   240
17   220
18   23B 4+
19   24B 3+   210 just to R.
20   25B 5-
21   26B 4
22   27B 4+   27b 4
23   28B 4
24   29B 4
25   310
26   30B 3+
27   320
28   340
29   16R 6b R to L
30   31B 5-
31   300
32   290
33   280
34   270
35   350
36   17R 5+
37   32B 4   32b 5+
38   18R 5
39   360
40   14Y

41   370
42   20R 5-
43   34B 4
44   19R 4+
45   380
46   21R 5-
47   390
48   35B 5-   35b 5+ Just to L.
49   22R 5+
50   33B 4
51   Traverse ?
52   38B 4-
53   39B 4+

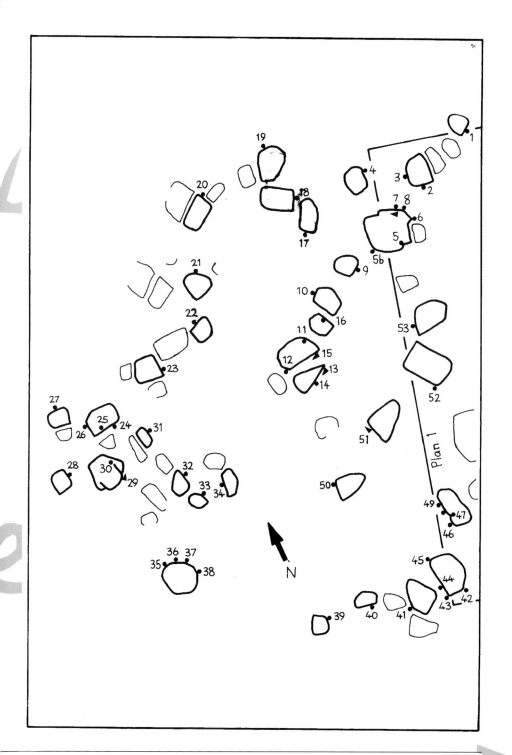

DIRECTIONS

Approaching from the north on the D409 (the main Fontainebleau/Milly-la-Forêt road) take the turn (just over 2kms west of the A6) heading SW signposted Noisy-sur-Ecole and La Musardière campsite. After about 1km park on the side of the road near an ONF barrier which blocks a track that leads eastward into the forest. Approaching from the other direction the parking is about 1km after La Musardière campsite.

WARNING: IN THE PAST INSENSITIVE PARKING HAS CAUSED ACCESS PROBLEMS AT THIS MASSIF SO PARK CAREFULLY.

Follow the track for about 130m before cutting up the hillside to the L just after the fence to find the problems.

CHARACTER

Open and quick drying with good views.

CLIMBING

There used to be BLUE and RED circuits here. Both have been more or less rubbed out by irrate locals (?) due to the above mentioned access problems. However, paint or no paint the boulder problems still exist and some of them are very fine. Two in particular deserve a mention; **Rubis sur l'Ongle 7b+** is one of the classics of the forest, a superb fingery problem up a fine, gently overhanging wall If you can climb Font 7b+ it's an essential tick. Just to its L is a hard eliminate; Gospel 7c+/8a depending on your method. They're in a corridor, you can't miss them.

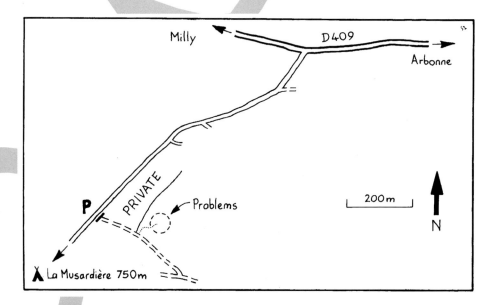

FRESH & FRUITY
ON THE EDGE T-SHIRTS & VESTS

TOTALLY WIRED

£12.95

oth designs feature
ON THE EDGE
ront left chest print

Colours:

T- Shirts - **Bottle Green,**

Navy Blue, Burgundy, Natural

Vests: **Ash, Black**

Sizes: **M,L,XL**

the perfect gift!

HAPPY CRANKER
£12.95

ORDER DETAILS

	T-SHIRT	VEST	SIZE	COLOUR
houlder Print	☐	N/A	☐	☐
tally Wired	☐	☐	☐	☐
appy Cranker	☐	☐	☐	☐

me (Caps)_____

dress (Caps) _____

_____ Postcode _____ Tel No._____

nclose my cheque/postal order for £_____ Payable To GreenShires Publishing

ease debit my: SWITCH (ISSUE No.) MASTERCARD VISA Expiry Date

y card number is

rdholder's name and address if different from above

me (Caps)_____

dress (Caps) _____

_____ Postcode _____ Tel No._____

ND TO : ON THE EDGE MAGAZINE, GREENSHIRES PUBLISHING, TELFORD WAY, KETTERING. NORTHANTS. NN16 8UN. UK

DIRECTIONS

From Fontainebleau take the D409 direction Milly-la-Forêt. 2 kms after crossing the A6 motorway turn left following signs for Noisy-sur-Ecole. After approx. 2 kms (soon after La Musardière campsite) turn left direction la Croix St Jérome. Straight on at the Croix, then left and immediately right, down a dirt track. Park at the end.

From Milly-la-Forêt follow the D16 direction Nemours. After approx. 2.5 kms turn left direction la Croix St Jérome - then as above.

95.2

From the carpark follow le Chemin de la Vallée Close eastwards keeping left where it forks. Once in the broad sandy plain of la Vallée Close keep to its right. A sandy path soon cuts up the hillside on the right at 90°. This leads to plan 1. The first problem faces north, a few metres to the R of the path as you near the crest of the pignon.

Les Gros Sablons

Stay on the right side of la Vallée Close following a smaller path that skirts the foot of the 95.2 pignon. At a small crossroads either (blue and black) turn R sticking to the foot of 95.2 and continue for about 50m until a wide sandy track crosses the path. Cross it and keep straight on (you are now on le Chemin du Pied des Monts). After approx. 300m another broad track cuts in from the right. The start of the black and blue circuits can be seen in the trees up to the left. Approx. 20 mins from parking. Or (oranges) go straight on to negotiate a maze of interconnecting paths and find the starts of the circuits of to the L and R. You may have to search a little!

CHARACTER

95.2

A beautiful massif, open and quick drying. Charismatically named after the altitude of the pignon, it's badly affected by erosion and is currently the object of an anti-erosion scheme undertaken by the Office National des Forêts in cooperation with the COSIROC. PLEASE RESPECT EFFORTS TO REDUCE EROSION IN THE MASSIF otherwise your mate will get squashed one day when a boulder loses its balance! Can get very hot in summer. A superb venue on cold, clear winter days, when, especially after a spell of poor weather, it can be extremely busy.

Les Gros Sablons

Another superb spot with good views over the Trois Pignons and some excellent picnic spots (Up on the top on plans 1 and 3). Dries fairly fast but lichen can make finishes nasty after rain. Never busy.

CLIMBING

95.2

Very popular with all levels of difficulty catered for. A handful of brilliant and hard unmarked problems. With a few glaring exceptions landings are good.

Two fun easy circuits west of the problems in the plans...

Yellow PD (54 problems)

Orange AD+ (50 problems)

And three harder classics, the white being particularly fine and very hard on the fingers...

Blue D (38 problems)

Red D+/TD- (47 problems)

White ED- (37 problems)

Les Gros Sablons

Orange no. 2 AD (40 problems) A good circuit with a fine finish.

Orange no. 1 AD+ (73 problems) This very fine, exhausting and varied expedition gives a big day out! Some bold problems for the colour.

Blue D+ (52 problems) Long and varied with a wide range of difficulty.

Black ED- (35 problems) A classic hard circuit with a reputation for boldness. A brilliant finalé on the 'crack' of la Liberté. Very fingery and some problems it's best not to fall from.

For those who want something a little more obscure there is also **le Rocher des Souris**, **le**

Rocher de Jean de Vignes and **les Rochers des Potets**. The first two are situated on the pignon nearest the carpark, on the south side of the path.

Where le Chemin de la Vallée Close forks, there's an obvious boulder off to the R (south) with some fun and games to be had on a roof. Up and a litte R there is...

1 **Prouesse 7b** The small but perfectly formed prow has a desperate start, especially for shrimps.

Further round to the R at more or less the same level, is...

2 **Oxygène Actif 7b**, a good R to L traverse. This is best reached via the small path that cuts of R about 100m after the carpark. The boulder is at the limit of the burnt and the unburnt ground.

If you follow the path that skirts the foot of the pignon (which eventually takes you to the Trois Pignons centre carpark), on its south side you'll see some boulders near the path.
This is...

Jean des Vignes

Blue D (35 problems) A very quiet circuit with some fine problems. There are also several unmarked traverses here. The best are probably:..

Simili Poutre 7b/c R to L on the bloc of the 5B, finishing L of the 5t blue

And down to the L, a little lower down...

Orage 7b L to R

Rouleau Divers 6c/7a R to L on the bloc of the 6B

Le Pierrot Lunaire 7b+ R to L. Finish up the 30B

E of Jean des Vignes and SW of 95.2 is a quiet, open massif with two excellent beginner's circuits.

Les Rochers des Potets

Yellow PD (42 problems)

Orange AD ((36 problems)

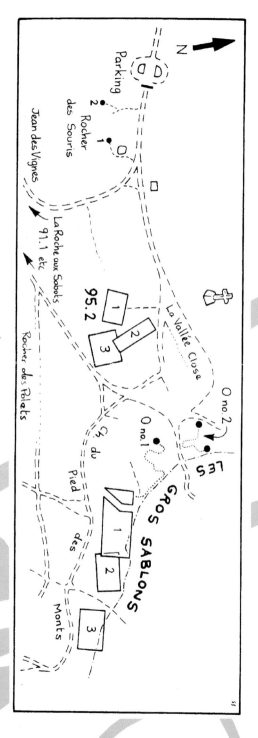

1 **Pierre Précieuse 6c+** static (think about it!), **7a+** dynamic. Jug to poor slope/crimp on R. Beautiful.

2 **38B 4+** END Blue

3 37B 3

4 **24W 5+**. Arete stepping R. Chipped wall to R gives a hard 6b.

5 **34B 4+**

6 **47R 5+** Sting in the tail! END Red

7 **Futurs Barbares 7c+**. Wall to L. Very powerful; precise footwork and strong fingers may get you to jug on 6. Few repeats.

8 25W 6a

9 36B 3+

10 26W 5

11 35B 4

12 33B 3+

13 32B 4+

14 27W 5

15 46R 4+

16 **28W 5**

17 28bW 7b Slab with desperate start.

18 45R 5

19 44R 5

20 43R 5

21 31B 3+

22 30B 3+

23 29B 4-

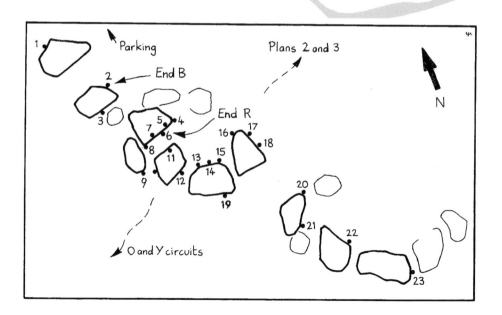

1   23W 5
2   **1R 4-**   START Red
3   **22W 5**
4   2R 4
5   21W 5-
6   3R 4+
7   4R 4
8   5R 4+
9   19W 6a
10 18W 6b
11 17W 5+
12 6R 4+
13 **16W 5**
14 **15W 5-**
15 7R 4
16 8R 3+
17 9R 4+
18 10R 4+
19 11R 5
20 **14W 5-**
21 12R 4 12b 4
22 **12W 5+**
23 13R 4+
24 14R 4
25 13W 5
26 11W 5+
27 20B 3+
28 **10W 6a** Arrows are confusing. Go diagonally L to R for the 6a and be spotted.
29 21B 4
30 15R 4+
31 **8W 5** Much harder without the arete.
32 9W 5
33 19B 3+
34 18B 4
35 16R 5- Diagonnaly R to L 16b 5+ direct.
36 15B 4-
37 **16B 5+**
38 17R 5+
39 **7W 6a**

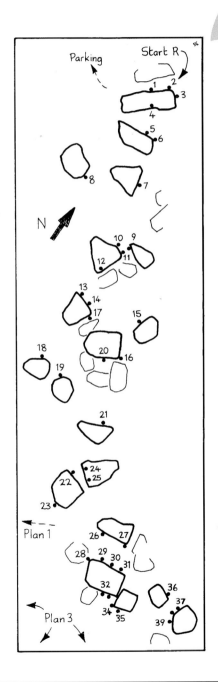

1 **1W Kilo de Beurre 5+** START White
2 32R 5
3 **Ange Naïf 7c+** Ahead-of-its-time dyno
with a static method as well.
4 **2W Le Poincenot 6c**
5 31R 4
6 2B 4-
7 1B 4   START Blue
8 29R 4+
9 28R 4+
10 4B 3+
11 30R 4
12 3B 4
13 **3W 5+**
14 3bW several games here. Two good-

ies... Direct to slopes on R is **6c.**
Diagonal L ward dyno to slope is
7a+.
15 5B 4+
16 6B 4
17 27R 5
18 7B 3
19 8B 4+
20 33R 4+ R to L
21 9B 4+
22 10B 4-
23 **35W 5**
24 35R 4+
25 34W 5+
26 36R 4-

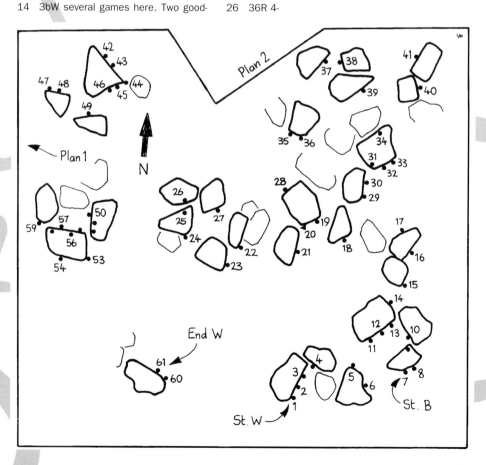

27 11B 4-
28 12B 4-
29 20R 4+
30 bW 7b
31 21R 4+
32 4W 6a
33 5W 6b
34 6W 5
35 13B 4+
36 23R 4 23b 5-
37 25R 5-
38 14B 3+
39 24R 4+
40 18R 4-
41 19R 5 L to R
42 22B 3
43 29W 5+ Up and L
29bW Mr Proper 7a Just to the L.
44 30W 6a
45 31W 5+

46 40R 5-
47 23B 4+
48 42R 5-
49 24B 4
50 33W 5+ 33b 6a
51 39R 4
52 25B 4
53 38R 4+
54 26B 3+
55 27B 4
56 32W Le Mur de la Fosse aux Ours 7a Lift off may be a problem!
57 37R 5-
58 32bW Danse avec les Loups 7b
59 28B 4- R to L
60 36W 5
61 37W 6b (direct) or **5+** leap L and back R. END White

Looking for a map, guide or book then why not take a look at our mountain library as featured in every issue of On The Edge, High and Summit magazines.

For help and information call GreenShires Publishing on **01536 525550** or write to us at Telford Way, Kettering, Northants, NN16 8UN.

We will be pleased to help you.

1   1B 5-   START Blue
2   1Bl La Popo 6b   START Black
3   2B 4+
4   3B 3+
5   4B 5
6   5B 4- 5b 5-
7   2Bl La Mandarine 5+ Direct is 6b.
8   200 2
9   230 3+
10 3Bl La Râpeuse 5
11 6B 4-
12 240 3+
13 7B 4+
14 260 3-
15 Unclimbed
16 10B 4+
17 Old peg route.
18 280 4-
19 4Bl La Piscine 5+
20 5Bl L'Expolivet 6a
21 6Bl La Toile Cirée 4+
22 300 4-
23 7Bl L'Oubliée5
24 10Bl La Colique 5 1m L **Dix sur Dix 7b**
25 12B 4+
26 9Bl 5 Odd. Step off adjacent bloc, swing R
    along top before mantel. Or... wall below is
    l'Oeil du Cyclone 7a.
27 320 3+
28 8Bl La Tête 4+
29 13B 4
30 330 2+
31 14B 3+
32 11Bl La Main Basse 5+
33 360 4-
34 15B 5+ 15b 4+
35 16B 4
36 12Bl La Brosse à Dents 5+
37 13Bl L'Iguane 5

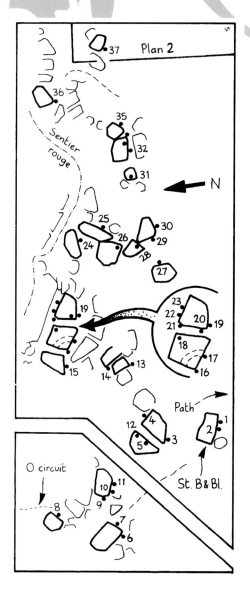

1   20B 4+
2   21B 4
3   15Bl L'Anti-Lerch 5+ Up and L. The fine, orange, marbled wall to the R has yet another neglected JP Bouvier desperate: **la Voie du Ciel 8a** (top rope).
4   14Bl Gueule d'Enfer 5+
5   Casus Belli 7a+
6   24B 5+
7   25B 4+
8   6c
9   26B 5+ L to R **26b 5**
10 450 3-
11 27B 4
12 17Bl Le Croque Monsieur 5+
13 18Bl La Didi 7a

14 29B 4+ 29b 3
15 480 3-
16 19Bl La Fusée 5
17 30B 3+
18 20Bl Le Treuil 4+
19 31B 3+
20 21Bl Le Bivouac 5+ Hard project to the L.
21 490 La Salle à Manger 2+
22 32B 4+
23 Project?
24 23Bl Le Suppositoire 6b
25 22Bl L'Everest 6a
26 33B 4+
27 530 3+
28 34B 5+

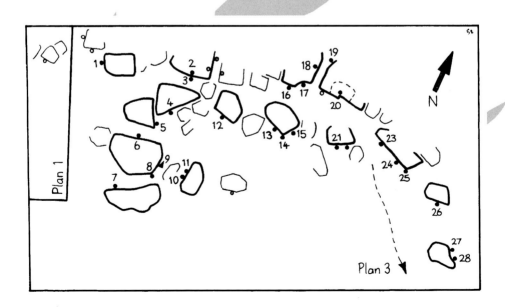

1 35B 5
2 550 2+
3 24BI La Patinoire 6a
4 570 3+
5 580 3
6 37B 5+
7 38B 4- 38b 5
8 39B 4
9 40B 4
10 41B 5+
11 42B 5-
12 43B 4-
13 31BI Les Parallèles 5
14 650 3
15 27BI La Possible 4+
16 640 Le Coup de Sabre 4
17 26BI 5
18 48B 4+
19 590 3+
20 47B 4- 47b 5   END Blue
21 25BI Le Hachoir 5+ 25b 6a

22 600 4- 60b 2+ 60t 4-
23 30BI La Chauve Souris 5
24 50B 5/5+
25 580 3
26 32BI 5-
27 33BI L'Ordure 5
28 710 3+ 71b 3+ 71t 3+
29 52B 3+ 52b 4
30 620 4
31 34BI Bande Première 6b
32 730 Les Trois Trous du Gruyère 3-
                          END Orange no. 1
33 51B 4
34 29BI L'Angle Gauche 5 R side of arete
Cherie J'ai Retraici 7a.
35 45B 4-
36 35BI La Pipicaca 6b   END Black
37 35bBI La Liberté 6b Sometimes referred
to as a crack but you'd be hard pushed to
jam it. Best 6b in the forest?
38 28BI L'Escalier 5+

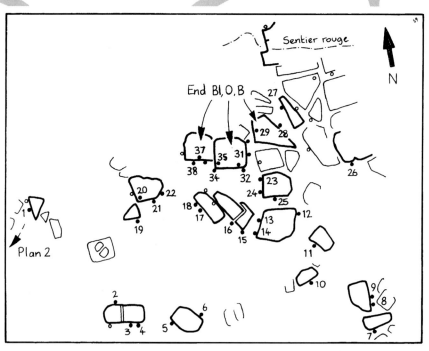

Nell Pearsons on Holey Moley 7a,
Cuvier. Richard Heap

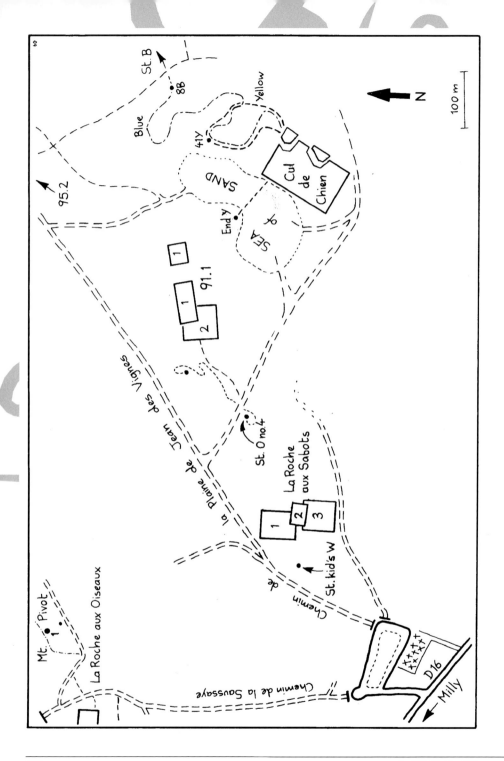

DIRECTIONS

Take the D16 south from Milly, direction Nemours. The carpark is on the L next to the cemetery, visible from the road after 4kms.

La Roche aux Oiseaux

Take the Chemin de la Saussaye for about 600m. The rocks are visible off to the L.

La Roche aux Sabots

For the children's circuit take the Chemin de la Plaine de Jean de Vignes. The circuit starts off to the R after about 180m. For the blue continue a little further and turn R into the woods where the track forks. For the start of the red take the R hand path from the carpark for about 200m. The boulders are on your L.

91.1

Take the Chemin de la Plaine de Jean de Vignes for about 450m. Turn R onto a broad sandy path. The start of the orange no.4 is soon after in the boulders on the R. For the main area turn L up the slope, following a small path past oranges and trend R to arrive at the 31R (no. 38, plan 2).

Le Cul de Chien

As for 91.1 but continue along the sandy path until dropping down L into 'la Mer du Sable'. At 'le Bilboquet', the characteristic rock in the middle, the problems are over to the R.

CHARACTER

La Roche aux Oiseaux

Shady and cool in summer, this very quiet and esoteric little massif dries slowly in winter. Be careful "Private" has been painted on some rocks where no access problems existed before.

La Roche aux Sabots

Small, compact massif. Can get extremely busy. Slow drying.

91.1 & Cul de Chien

Beautiful, open massifs which dry quickly. Can get very busy in autumn and winter but best avoided in a heatwave.

CLIMBING

La Roche aux Oiseaux

A handful of superb problems and plenty of others to warm up on. The better problems are pretty high and some haven't been done without a rope (yet). Some may need a brush.

Nearby is Mont Pivot. On its SE flank, just below the ridge and the path you will find the brilliant and totally obscure...

1 Belle Gueule 6c An overhanging pocketed wall. Almost directly below this at the foot of the pignon is a superb slab with an undercut start.

La Roche aux Sabots

A superb area with something for everyone. Good landings in general.

White (children's) Well marked and fun.

Yellow PD+ (33 problems) Excellent circuit; varied and technical.

Blue D (46 problems) As above. One of the best circuits of its grade in the forest.

Red TD- (34 problems) Another minor masterpiece with more strenuous, technical problems than you could possibly hope for (and a couple of slab stoppers).

91.1

Yellow PD+ (50 problems) Good beginner's circuit.

Orange no. 4 AD- (37 problems) Popular, varied circuit.

Orange no. 2 AD+ (51 problems) Ditto

Red TD- (34 problems) Fine, technical circuit, more delicate than strenuous. Some high problems and/or bad landings.

Le Cul de Chien

Very popular area with friendly landings.

Yellow PD (58 problems) Long, varied classic.

Blue D (53 problems) Interesting and varied. The first 50 or so problems (quieter as a rule) are worth seeking out (see Trois Pignons centre area map).

Red TD/TD+ (30 problems) Some excellent problems but best known for its famous roof.

1 La fastoche 4
2 La cent blagues 5+
3 La tire à gauche 5
4 Le rossignol 5-
5 Le rouge gorge 5
6 Le pigeon 5-
7 La fauvette 5
8 L'autruche 5-
9 Le flamand rose 5+
10 Le cygne 5+
11 L'oiseau lyre 5+
12 Loi sauvage 5+
13 Le vilain petit canard 5+
14 6b
15 Action directe 6c
16 L'Anarchronique 7a (With a loop near the start – 7c.)
17 La cuit cuit 6a
18 La Chouette 6c
19 Le Grand Duc 6b

20 Hibou lugubre 5+
21 La tire au cul 5-
22 La tire à vue 4
23 Triple buse 5+
24 Le coucou 5
25 Prise de bec 6a
The climbs in the corridor are fine and terrifying and you should bring a rope.
26 La tourterelle 6a
27 L'Aigle Royal 6b
28 L'albatros 6c
29 Le Saut du Nid 6a
30 Le Pinçon 6a
La Révolution du Silence 7b is the overhanging arete round to the L of the big slabs in the corridor.
31 Project?
Now you're fully warmed up and in the mood for esoterica nip round to Mont Pivot and try **Belle Gueule 6c.**

Sam Whittaker on Le Toit
du Cul de Chien 6c/7a.
Paul Higginson

1	1B 3+	START Blue
2	2B 3+	
3	20Y 2+	
4	3B 4	
5	4B 4	Round to L 21Y.
6	**5B 4-**	
7	**13R 5-**	
8	**14R 6b** 14b Lime à Ongles 6c	
9	**6B 4**	
10	**7B 4+**	
11	**15R 6a** L to R. A low variant exists 7a/b	
12	8B 3-	
13	**9B 5-**	
14	22Y 2+	
15	10B 4-	
16	11B 3	
17	**15bR Lucifer 7b** Short, intense slab on tiny holds.	
18	**17bR 6c** Overhanging arete.	
19	**12B 4+**	
20	**Déviation 7c+/8a+** Direct from the ground is possible (for Marc le Menestrel at least) but utterly desperate. Most use a stone to start. Other games here, **Le Bond de l'Hippopotame** steps L from the 12B and leaps to the top. Ungradeable.	
21	**17R 5-**	
22	13B 3	
23	14B 3+	
24	15B 4-	
25	25Y 3 25b 3	
26	16B 4+	
27	17B 4+	
28	18B 5 18b 5-	
29	**17tR Ras du Q 6c** Exit via crack. **L'Anglomaniaque 6c** starts round to the R to finish up Ras du Q.	
30	**Miss World 7c** L to R	
31	**19B 4**	
32	**12R 5+**	
33	**11R 6a**	
34	**10R 5**	
35	19Y 2+	
36	20B 4+	
37	24Y 3-	
38	18Y 1+	
39	21B 4+	
40	**22B 4+**	
41	**23B 5-**	
42	18bR Le Toit Chinois 6b	
43	27Y 2	
44	17Y 2	
45	24B 3+	
46	**18R 5+** Hard to start. The aretes on either side can be done with a dyno from the ground: L side 6c/7a, R side 7a+ (morpho).	
47	25B 3+	
48	28Y 2	
49	26B 4	
50	**19R 5+**	
51	16Y 2	
52	**9R 5-**	
53	15Y 3	
54	14Y 2+	
55	29B 4+	

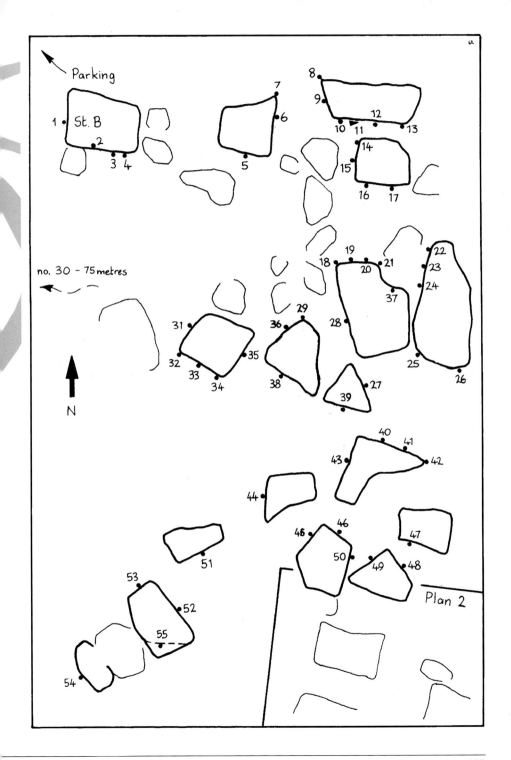

1 **20tR Amanite Dalloïde 7a**
2 **20bR Bazooka Jo 6b**
3 **20R 5**
4 **27B 5-**
5 28B 3+
6 29Y 2-
7 21R 5
8 **22R 5+**
9 **23R 5** Starting low to the R is fun
10 **24R 5+**
11 **24bR A l'Impossible Nul n'est Tenu 7a**
   (aka L'Epluche Patate). This steep slab is
   superb, very fingery and hard even for the
   best.
12 **25R 6b**
13 30B 3+ 30b 5-

14 **26R 5**
15 **27R 5+**
16 **28R 6a**
17 **29R 6b**
18 30Y 3
19 31B 3+
20 **30R 5-**
21 31R 5-
22 **32R 5**
   Rumsteak en Furie 6c/7a The entire bloc
   L to R.
23 33R 5
24 34B 4
25 33B 4+
26 31Y 2   31b 3-   END Yellow
27 32B 4

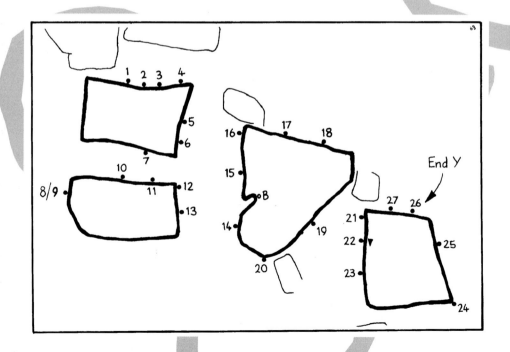

The UK's Favourite Climbing Magazines

The High Info pages are invaluable as a reference either for getting information for expeditions or for researching articles or books".

Chris Bonnington.

"On the Edge is everything I look for in a climbing partner, funny sexy and it knows all the right moves. I get it every month"

Ben Moon.

"For a representative body, good communication is vital. BMC Summit id how we reach all our members with news and information that protects their interests as climbers, hillwalkers and mountaineers and helps them get the most from their activities".

Roger Payne, General Secretary of the BMC.

"High Magazine, informative, accurate .... an entertaining read".

Joe Simpson.

FOR FURTHER INFORMATION PLEASE CONTACT GILL WOOTTON OR ALISTAIR CROOKES

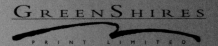

GREENSHIRES
PRINT LIMITED

Telford Way, Kettering, Northamptonshire NN16 8UN
Telephone: 01536 525550 Facsimilies: 01536 522621 Email; greenshires@atlas.co.uk Internet: www.greenshires.com

1	**1R 5+**	START Red
2	**2R 5**	
3	**3R 6a**	

3b **3bR Le Tourniquet 7a** Traverse the entire boulder L to R.

4	4R 5	
5	2Y 3-	
6	**Parti de Jambes en l'Air 7b** R to L.	
7	3Y 2	
8	39B 4-	
9	4Y 1+	
10	40B 4-	
11	**5bR Le Graviton 7b**	

12 **Sale Gosse 7c** Standing start and one almighty lunge for the top. Low start is **7c+/8a?**

13	**5R 5**	
14	5Y 3-	
15	**41B 3+**	
16	6Y 2+	
17	**43B 4**	
18	42B 4+	
19	7c R to L - exit just L of arete.	
20	**6R 5**	

6bR Achille Talon 6c
Two problems between 20 and 21
R is Jus d'Orange 7a
L is 100% Pulpe 7b

21	**7R 4+**	
22	7Y 3	
23	8Y 2+	
24	10Y 1+	
25	11Y 2-	
26	12Y 3-	12bY 3
27	**8R 5**	
28	9Y 3	9bY 3
29	44B 4-	
30	45B 5-	
31	**46B 4**	END Blue
32	13Y 2+	
33	35B 3+	
34	36B 4	
35	37B 3+	
36	34bR Le Surplomb des Frelons 6c	

La Traversée des Frelons 6c+. Start R of 36B. Exit up le Surplomb.

37	38B 4	
38	1Y 2+	START Yellow
39	**34R 5**	END Red

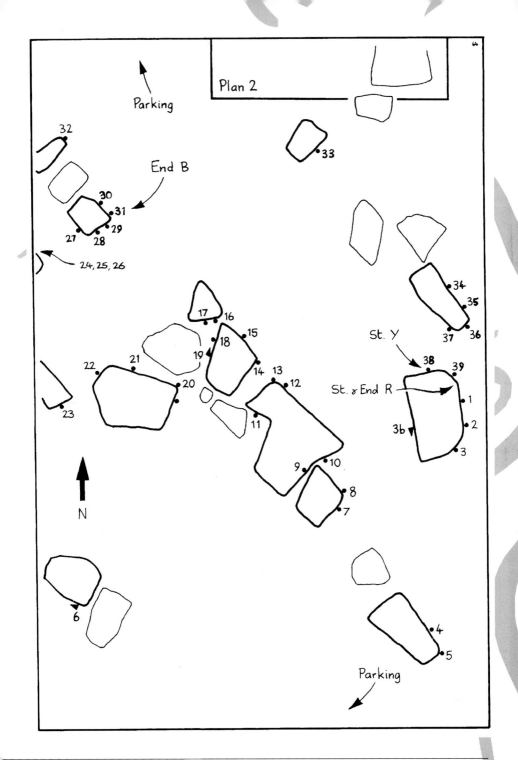

1 10 3-   START Orange no. 1
2 20 3-
3 30 3+
4 40 3+ The red problem just to the L is **6b.**
5 50 4
6 60 3+
7 70 3
8 80 3+ 8b 4
9 90 3
10 100 3+
11 110 3
12 1R 4+   START Red
13 2R 5   **2b 5/6b** L side of arete is height dependent and much harder static.
14 3R 3+
15 120 4-
16 130 4-
17 140 3+
18 150 3-
19 4R 4-
20 5R 4   5b 5+
21 160 4-
22 6R 4-   6b 4+
23 170 2+
24 7R 5
25 180 2+
26 190 4+
27 200 3-
28 210 3
29 220 3
30 230 3
31 8R 4+   8b 6a
32 240 4-
33 250 3+
34 9R 5-   9b 5+
35 10R 4   10b 5+ Round to the R.
36 260 4

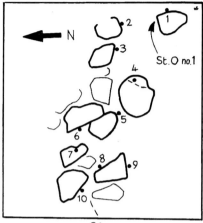

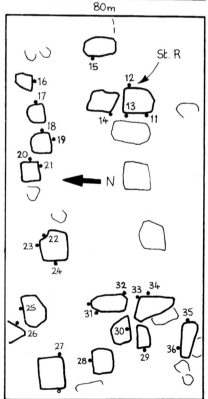

80m

Jacques le Menestrel on
Gnossienne 7c, Isatis.
Alain Hoffman

1   270 3+
2   11R 4 11b4
3   280 4-
4   12R 5+ L of the 12R there's a fingery
eliminate 7a.
5   12tR 5+
6   12bR L'Arc de Cercle 5
7   290 3-
8   13R 4+/5+ Easier stepping L
9   48Y   END Yellow
10 14R 6a 14b 5-
11 300 3+
12 310 3+
13 15R 5   15b 5-
14 16R 5   16b 5+
15 320 3
16 17R 4+
17 18R 5-
18 330 3-
18b 6a The fine overhanging prow. Top-roped
normally but impressive more than hard.
19 19R 5-
20 20R 4
21 21R 4-
22 340 2+
23 22R 4+
24 350 3-
25 23R 5   23b 5+
26 370 3
27 24R 4+
28 25R 4+ 25b 5-
29 26R 4+ 26b 5+
30 380 2
31 400 3-
32 36Y
33 27R 4+
34 410 3+
35 28R 4
36 29R 5
37 30R 5
38 31R 4 31b 5-
39 420 3-
40 430 3
41 32R 5- 32b 4+
42 6c/7a R to L Exit up L arete.

43 33R 4+ **33b 6b** R of the bis, just L of the
R arete is a tricky problem.
44 440 3
45 450 3
46 460 3
47 470 3
48 480 3+
49 490 4
50 34R 5+   END Red
51 500 4
52 510 4+   END Orange

LE CUL DE CHIEN Plan 1

1	1R 5-	START Red
2	2R 5-	
3	3R 5+	
4	**50B 4+**	END Blue
5	4R 5	
6	49B 3+	
7	48B 4	
8	5R 4/5	

9 Le Toit du Cul de Chien 6c/7a
Perhaps the forest's most famous problem, this is an essental rite of passage for all aspiring bleausards. Freed in 1978, arguments about the grade will go on forever. Several methods, the easiest of which involves (as usual) crafty footwork. The oddest gets the pocket on the lip R handed. Ambitious project wants to go R into...

10 Le Toit aux Grattons 7a+/7b This painful, rarely climbed variant has a nasty fall if fingers zip. Reach out L from 11.

11 6R La Nano 6a

12 7R 6a Excellent arete, more L than R.

13 8R 5

14 28B 4-

15 9R 5

16 10R 5

17 27B 4-

18 11R 5+

19 12R 5-

20 47B 4-

21 13R 4

22 14R 5+

23 15R 5+ L to R

24 16R 5

25 17R 5

26 18R 5+ R to L to tricky finish.

27 19R 5-

28 20R 4+

29 44B

30 21R 5+

31 43B

The winter and spring of '96/'97 saw several excellent new additions to this well hidden boulder...

32 L'Autre Toit 7b "The other roof" of the dog's bottom is the original problem of the bloc. Standing start from obvious holds. Exits direct.

The Integral 8a+ has a crouching start at the back. Very powerful. Finishes up L'Autre Toit.

Eclipse to the L reaches into the obvious flared crack from the R. Standing start with or without the embedded stone 7b+ and 7cish respectively. Eclipse can be joined from L'Autre Toit at 7cish.

L'Oeil de la Sybille 7c+ is 2m R of L'Autre Toit.

33	40B 3+	
34	41B 3+	
35	42B 3-	
36	22R 6a	
37	**22bR Hammer's Break 6c/7a**	
38	23R 5+ Between 23 & 24R is an old blue 5-	
39	**24R 4+**	
40	25R 4+	
41	26R 5-	
42	27R 5/6a	
43	28R 6a	
44	29R 5-	
45	**30R 5-**	END Red

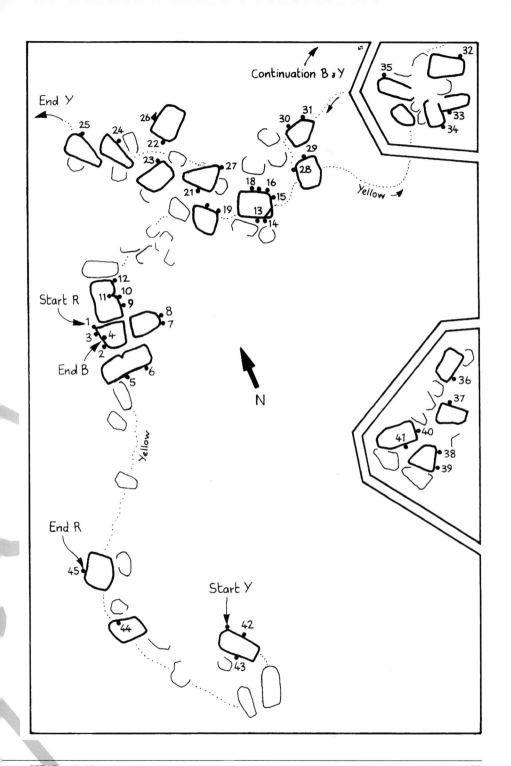

Continuation B & Y

End Y

Start R

End B

End R

Start Y

N

Yellow

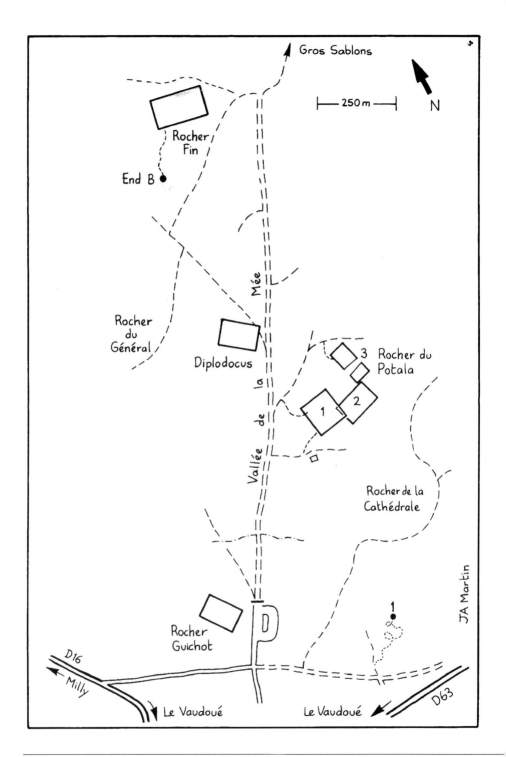

Gros Sablons

├── 250 m ──┤

N

Rocher Fin

End B

Mée

Rocher du Général

Diplodocus

Vallée de la

3 Rocher du Potala

1 2

Rocher de la Cathédrale

Rocher Guichot

1

JA Martin

D16

Milly

Le Vaudoué

Le Vaudoué

D63

DIRECTIONS

From Milly take the D16 south, direction Nemours. The turn for the carpark is on the L 1 km after the Trois Pignons centre carpark (cemetery), 500m before the le Vaudoué crossroads.

Rocher Guichot

As you enter the carpark it's on the L, barely 50m away.

Le Rocher du Potala

Take the main path for about 500/550m. Two possible R turns. The first, smaller path takes you to the start of the blue. The second, to the start of the red.

Diplodocus

About 750m from the carpark a small path cuts off obliquely to the L. Take it and the rocks are soon visible on the L.

Rocher Fin

Geographicaly this is part of Trois Pignons centre but access is easier from here. Just over 1.5 km from the carpark the path comes to a sort of T junction. Turn L and look for a small path that heads up the slope to the R. Take this for a short distance before heading off obliquely L to find the start of the blue and red circuits.

CHARACTER

Rocher Guichot

Very convenient but slower to dry than its neighbours.

Le Rocher du Potala

Quick drying. Can get very busy.

Diplodocus

Open and fairly quick drying. Very busy.

Rocher Fin

Mostly open and quick drying, a good spot in winter. The end of the blue dries more slowly. Avoid it in hot weather.

CLIMBING

Rocher Guichot

Yellow AD- (28 problems)
Blue D (20 problems)
Red TD+ (21 problems) Some painful holds.
Three good circuits at their respective grades.

Good landings.

Le Rocher du Potala

Orange AD/AD+ (40 problems)
Blue D (38 problems)
Red TD+ (48 problems) Another very crimpy red circuit.
Three excellent circuits with constant interest. Good landings. Le Surplomb makes a visit essential for very strong folk.

Diplodocus

Yellow PD (26 problems)
Orange AD (23 problems)
Blue D (23 problems)
Two excellent beginner's circuits and a blue with some interesting problems. Good landings although you'll need a long neck for the Diplodocus.

Rocher Fin

Yellow PD (13 problems) Short and difficult to follow.
Blue D (53 problems) Long and spread out. The best is saved for the end.
Red TD+ (34 problems) Yet more crimptastic horrors.
Good landings in general.

And if you want real peace and quiet try...

Le Rocher du Général

Just behind (NW) of Diplodocus.
Yellow PD (24 problems) Starts by the path at the foot of the pignon.
Blue D+ (30 problems) Starts higher up the pignon to the L. Quite spread out. Finishes on pignon to the north.

Rocher de la Cathédrale

Between JA Martin and le Rocher du Potala.
Orange AD+ (54 problems)

1 Jardin Secret 7b+ L to R traverse From the carpark take the Chemin du Rocher Cailleau for about 300m then go L into a small massif (see map) and walk around in circles until you find it. Graded for an exit extreme R but others possible, both easier and harder.

1	1B 4	START Blue
2	2B 4	
3	3B 4	
4	Project	
5	**1R 5**	START Red
6	**2R 6a**	
7	3R 6a	
8	**4R 6b**	
9	**5B 4+**	
10	6B 4+	
11	5R 6b+	
12	**6R 6a**	
13	7B 4	
14	8B 4+	
15	7R 6b	
16	8R 5+	
17	9B 5	
18	9R 5	
19	10B 5-	

20 11B 4 And down in the hole to the R is Mayonnaise de Passion 7b+/7c R to L under roof to finish up weakness.
L'Univers des Arts 7c L to R starts L of 11bB to finish through roof.

21	12B 5
22	**13B 4+**
23	?
24	10R 6a
25	11R 5+
26	**12R 5+**
27	**13R 5+**
28	**14R 5+**
29	**14B 5**
30	15B 4+
31	**15R 6a**
32	**16R 6b**
33	**17R 6a** Up and L
34	16B 4+
35	**18R 5**
36	17B 5 L to R
37	18B 5
38	**19B 4+**
39	**19R 6b**
40	20R 6a

41 **21R 6c** if done from lip, harder if done from the back   END Red

42 **6c** Jump to edge.

43 **5** L along break from 20B then leap or crank to jug.

44 **20B 5**   END Blue

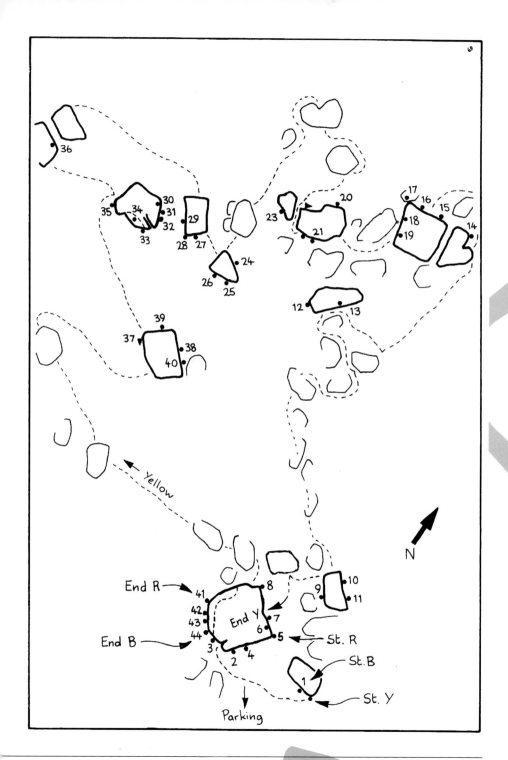

1	**1R 5-**	START Red
2	2R 5-	
3	**3R 5-**	
4	**4R 5+**	
5	**5R 5+**	
6	**6R 6a**	
7	7R 5	
8	8R 6a 8bR 6b L to R and up 8.	
9	9R 5- Just to the L 9bR 5+	
10	**10R 5+**	

11	**1B 4+**	START Blue
12	**11R Les Trois Lancers 5**	
13	12R 5+	
14	13R 5+ Just L of arete 2bB 5	
15	**2B 4**	
16	**14R 5**	
17	**15R 6b**	
18	16R 5	
19	**17R 5+** Harder from the back.	
20	18R 5 L to R	

21	4B 3+
22	5B 3+
23	**19R La Voie Lacquée 6b**
24	6B 4
25	7B 5-
26	8B 4+
27	9B 4-
28	10B 4-
29	20R 6a
30	**21R La Clef de Pie 5**
31	11B 3+
32	12B 4
33	22R La Contorsion 5
34	12bB 4

Le Rocher du Potala plan 2

1	13B 4-
2	14B 4-
3	23R 5
4	30 3+
5	40 4- R to L
6	60 3+ R to L
7	**15B 4**
8	**50 4-**

9	24bR 5	
10	15bB 4+	
11	24R 5+	
12	**20 3+**	
13	25R 5	
14	**26R 5-**	
15	27R 5-	
16	**10 3-**	START Orange
17	16B 3+ 16bB 4+	
18	**28bR 6b+**	
19	**28R 5+**	
20	7, 8 and 90 All 3ish.	
21	110 4	
22	100 3	
23	29R 5+	
24	30R 6b	
25	**31R 5+**	
26	32R 5+	
27	130 3+	
28	19B 4	
29	140 4-	
30	20B 4 and 33R 5-	
31	22B 3	
32	**34R 5**	

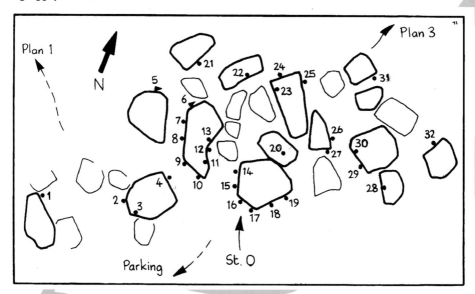

1 35R 5+
2 170 3
3 24B 4
4 220 3-
5 230 4-
6 240 3+
7 250 3-
8 36R 5-
9 37R 5+   Round corner: 37b 6a R to L
10 38R 6b
11 39R 5-
12 40R 5
13 360 3+
14 31B 4
15 R to L
16 370 3
17 41R 5
18 42R 5- 42bR 5+
19 43R La Fissure au Marbre 5
20 32B 4-
21 6b L to R to finish up 20
22 33B 4-
23 34B 4-
24 35B 4
25 44R 5-
26 380 4-
27 45R Les Petits Pieds 5+ R to L
28 46R 5
29 36B 3+
30 390 2+
31 37B 3
32 47R 5
33 400 3 R to L   END Orange
34 48R 6a   END Red
35 38B 4+   END Blue
36 **Le Surplomb de la Mée 8a+** Desperately
up to rounded undercut then up and L to a
tricky finish.
La Traversée de la Mée 7c+ A more
amenable alternative. Start up 38B then L
into undercut. Finish as for le Surplomb.
An alternative exit is to finish direct from
the undercut. 8a+ if done with the direct
start.

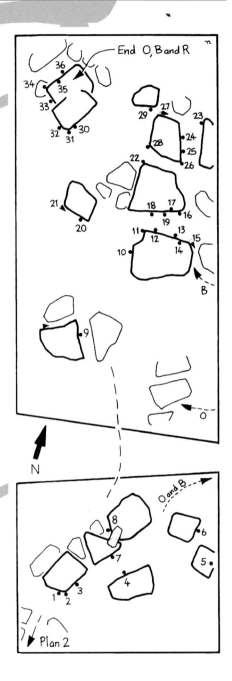

Pure friction!

Ben Moon and Jerry Moffatt on the ultimate bouldering road trip.....

.....to the sounds of Warp, The Lisa Marie Experience, Marmion, Atlantic Ocean, Grinstretcher, Progress, DJ Food, Coldcut, S-Bam and The Art of Trance

PRODUCTIONS

VIDEO DISTRIBUTION

NO FEAR

LDR Climbing Walls

BENDCRETE
BENDCRETE
BENDCRETE
CLIMBING WALLS

arnette

BOREAL

Please return coupon to: ON THE EDGE Magazine, Greenshires Publishing, Telford Way, Kettering, Northants NN16 8UN

Please return coupon to: **ON THE EDGE MAGAZINE,**
Greenshires Publishing, Telford Way, Kettering, Northants NN16 8UN

PLEASE SEND ME ☐ COPIES OF *"THE REAL THING"*
AT THE PRICE OF £16.00 EACH
(Please add Postage and Packaging: UK - £1.25, Overseas - £4.00)

I enclose a cheque for £_____ (made payable to: Greenshires Publishing
Please debit my credit card   *WE ACCEPT VISA/MASTERCARD/SWITCH*

EXPIRY DATE   **ISSUE NUMBER**

CARDHOLDER'S SIGNATURE

NAME

ADDRESS

POSTCODE   *DAYTIME TEL NO.*

ON THE EDGE MAGAZINE • THE REAL THING

DIPLODOCUS

1	1B 4	START Blue	**47**	**230 4**		END Orange
2	**10 3**	START Orange	**48**	**23B 4**	23b 4+	END Blue
3	2B 4					
4	20 3					
5	3B 4					
6	30 3+					
7	4B 3+					
8	40 2+					
9	50 4					
10	5B 4					
11	60 2+					
12	6B 4-					
13	7B 4					
14	70 4					
15	80 3					
16	8B 4					
17	90 3					
18	100 3-					
19	9B 4					
20	110 2					
21	120 3					
22	10B 4					
23	130 3+					
24	11B 4+					
25	12B 4+					
26	140 3+					
27	13B 4-					
28	15b0 3					
29	14B 5					
30	150 3					
31	15B 4					
32	160 3					
33	16B 4					
34	16b0 3					
35	17B 4+					
36	170 3					
37	18B 4					
38	19B 4					
39	180 2+					
40	190 3-					
41	20B 4+					
42	**200 2+**					
43	21B 4					
44	210 3+					
45	22B 3+	22b 4 the 'tooth' to the L.				
46	220 3					

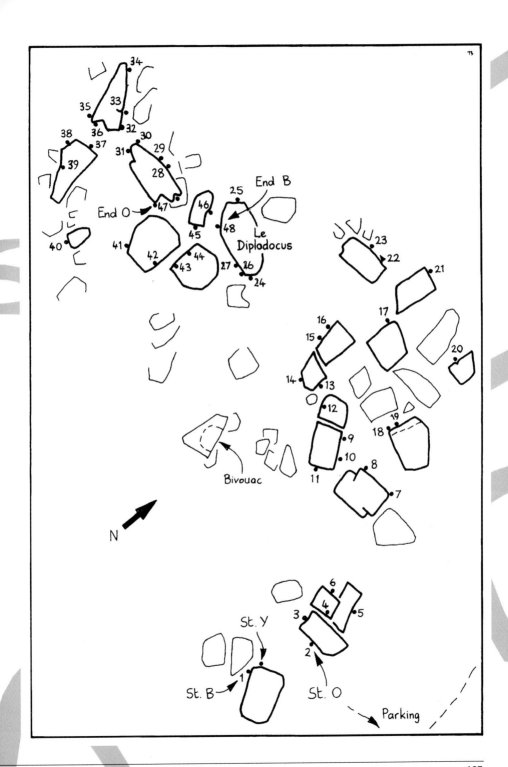

1	1B 4 R to L START Blue
2	**1R 5** Bold arete. START Red
3	**2R 5+** R to L + arete.
4	2B 4
5	3R 4+
6	3B 4 R to L
7	4B 4
8	**11R 5**
9	12R 4+
10	13R 5+ R to L
11	5B 3
12	6B 3+
13	7B 4
14	**8B 4+** Under the nose starting from the back is Mémoire d'Outre Tombe 7b, exit R.
15	**9B 4** R to L
16	10B 3
17	**11B 3+**
18	12B 4 L to R
19	13B 4+ L to R
20	**14R 5-**
21	**14B 4-**
22	**15B 4- 15b 4-**
23	15R 5
24	**16R 5+**
25	**Les Serbes 7b**
	Les Croates 7b is further R.
26	17R 5
27	**18R 5+**
28	19R 5+
29	**20R 6a**
30	**4+** Just to the L is the crack that marks the start of the yellow circuit.
31	21R 6a L to R
32	22R 6a
33	**23R 4+**
34	**24R 5**
35	**25R 5-**
36	17B 3+
37	18B 3+
38	26R 6b/c Steer well clear of this horror in summer (the same goes for most of the crimpy reds). Even in winter it's nigh on impossible...
39	**19B 4**
40	**27R 5+**

41	**28R 5**
42	**20B 3+**
43	21B 3+
44	22B 4 L to R
45	4R 4
46	5R 4+
47	**6R 5**
48	**7R 5+** R to L and up.
49	8R 4-
50	9R 5
51	10R 5
52	23B 3
53	**29R 5-**
54	**30R 5**
55	**31R 4+**
56	**32R 5 32b 5+**
57	24B 3+
58	33R 5
59	**34R 5+** END Red
60	16B 4
61	26B 3
62	27B 4
63	28B 3+
64	29B 3+

The blue circuit continues from here. It's a little spread out but fairly well marked. Some of nos. 42 to 53 (the end of the circuit) are excellent.

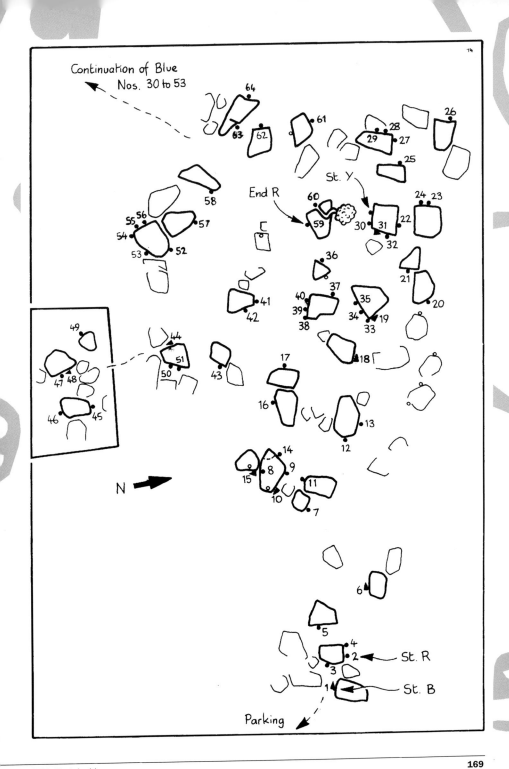

DIRECTIONS

From Milly follow the D16 south, direction Nemours as far as Le Vaudoué. Turn L onto the D63, direction Achères. The carpark is on the L just over a km further.

From Fontainebleau follow the D409 as far as Arbonne, then the D64 direction Achères. Turn R, direction le Vaudoué and the carpark is on the R after 2kms.

Most of the circuits start in or next to the sandy clearing 100m from the carpark. For the starts of the red and light blue circuits, cross the clearing and take the path that heads up the hill. The starts are on an obvious boulder on the L with a prominent corner crack.

CHARACTER

South facing, this excellent spot dries fairly quickly but can be very hot in summer. The variety of climbing offered means it can get busy but the massif is spread out enough for it to be possible to find a quiet spot.

CLIMBING

White (children's 38 problems)
Yellow PD- (54 problems)
2 Oranges, nos. 2 and 3, both AD+ (both 86 problems)
Light blue D- (38 problems?)
Blue D+ (36 problems?) Interesting and varied.
Red TD+ (48 problems?) Hard, crimpy and bold at times, this old classic has recently (summer 96) been re-worked.

Across the road from the carpark, about 80m into the woods is the aptly named...
1 Voyageur Solitaire 7b+ L to R

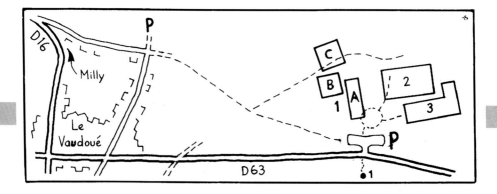

Here is the blue no.5 (3+ to 5) and some good orange problems.

One outstanding problem:

L'Etrave 7b (L of 21B, plan 1c). Success depends on your pain tolerance at the key crux crimp.

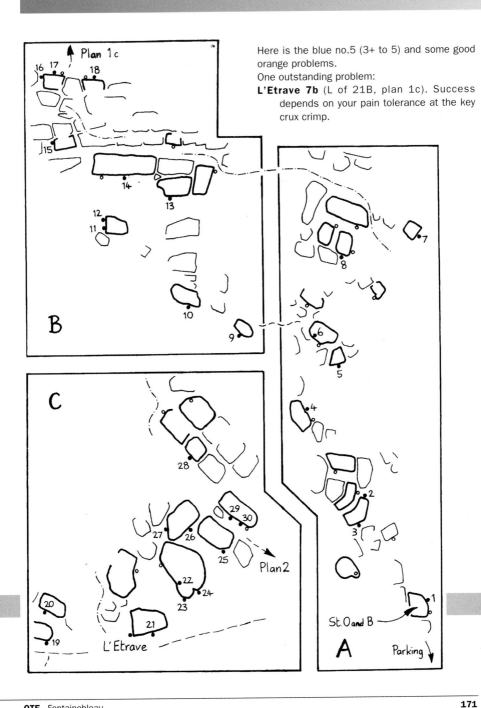

1 **1LB La Fissure de la Grand Mère 5**
   START Light Blue
2 **1R 6c** START Red
3 2R 5+
4 3LB 3+
5 **3R 5**
6 4LB 4+
7 **4R La Coquille 6a** The chipped holds are hardly discreet but this is still a classic.
8 5R 5
9 **6R 5**
10 **7R 5+** The crack. A 6c/7a zigzags up the wall to the L.
11 8R 5+ The wall opposite is **6b** and harder for shrimps.
12 9R 5 Good R to L into 9R from R arete **5+**
12a **7a** Weird move to obvious hold.
13 **5LB 4**
14 10R 5+
15 7LB 4 and 9LB 4
16 **11R 5+** 1.5 m L is Niaque way 7b.
17 10LB 3
18 2 The big diamond shaped slab is fun.
19 **11bLB La Truande 5**
20 12LB 4+
21 **12R 5+** L to R
22 860 3+ Down, L to R and arete.
   END Orange
23 6a?
24 6a
25 LB 3+
26 **19R 5** L to R
27 54Y 2 END Yellow
28 53Y 2 Down, R to L
29 13R 5
30 18R 6b
31 14R 6a
32 17R 5
33 15R 5
34 **LB 4-**
35 810 3 Down, R to L
36 **20R 6a**
37 **21R 5+** A traverse 8a, starts by the 19B to finish L of 21R.
38 **16R 5**
39 780 3-

40 800 3-
42 **22R 6a** R to L
43 **5+** The crack beside the bivouac.
44 43Y

Down the slope and a little to the L is the 23R 5 and on the same boulder, Aster 7c+, a L to R traverse.

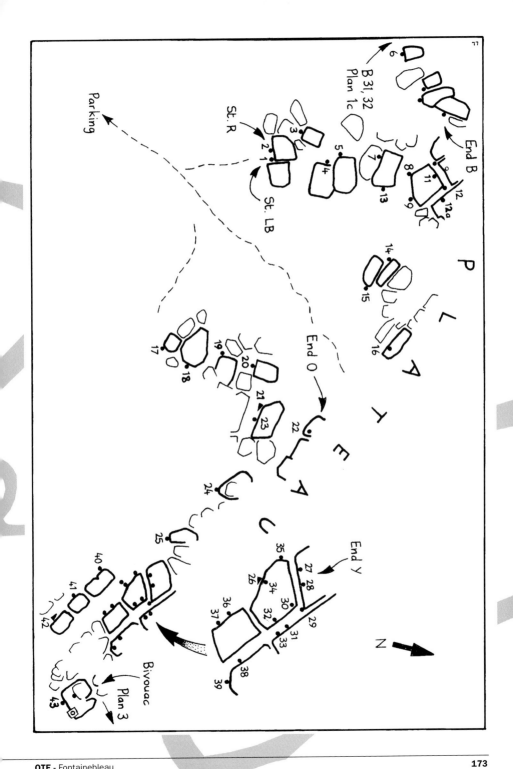

1 LB 3+
2 R 5
3 R 5+
4 R 5
5 LB 3+
6 LB 3+
7 LB 4-
8 R 5+
9 R 5+ L to R
10 LB 4+
11 R 5+
12 LB 3
13 LB 4
14 R 5+
15 LB 3-
16 R 5
17 R 6a
18 R 5+
19 LB 4
20 LB 3+
21 LB 3+
22 310 4R to L
23 R 5
24 LB 3+
25 R 5+
26 LB 3+
27 33R 5
28 34R 6a
29 LB 4
30 31R 6a
31 30R 5+
32 LB 4-
33 29R 5+
34 LB 3
35 24R 6a
36 110 4 with arete.
37 25R 5
38 26R 5+
39 28R 5+
40 27R 5+ L to R and up.
41 LB 3+
42 LB 3+
43 90 3+
44 70 3
45 LB 4
46 LB 4

END Light Blue

END Red

47 60 3+
48 LB 3
49 50 4-
50 40 2

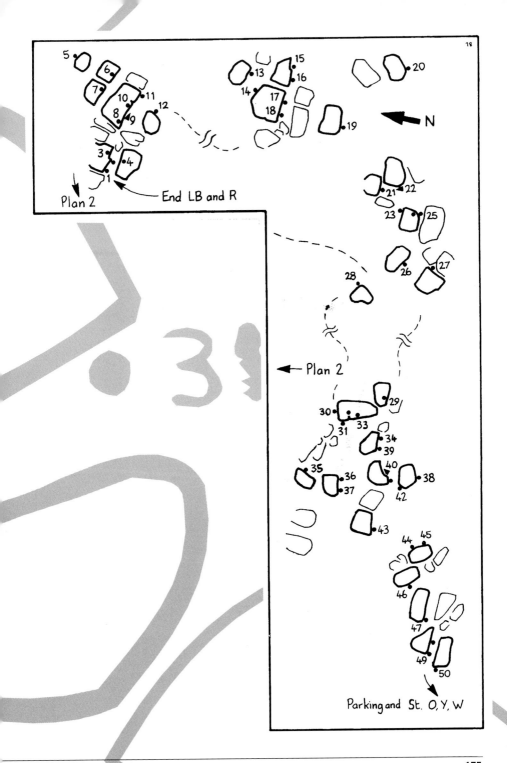

End LB and R

Plan 2

Plan 2

N

Parking and St. O, Y, W

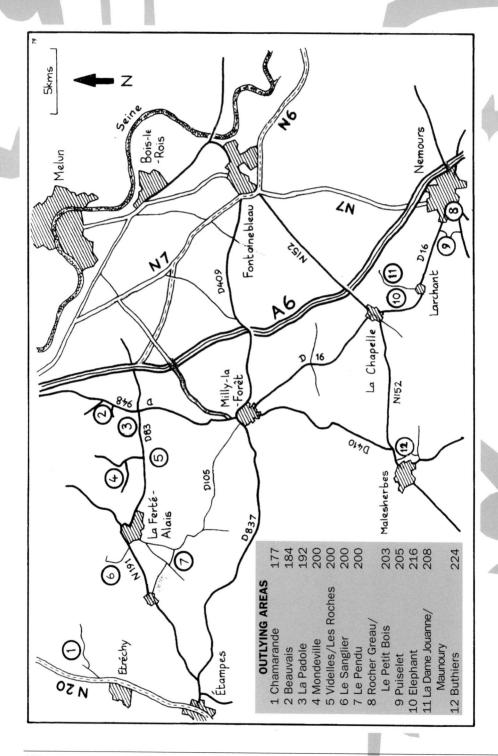

OUTLYING AREAS

1 Chamarande	177
2 Beauvais	184
3 La Padole	192
4 Mondeville	200
5 Videlles/Les Roches	200
6 Le Sanglier	200
7 Le Pendu	200
8 Rocher Greau/	
Le Petit Bois	203
9 Puiselet	205
10 Elephant	216
11 La Dame Jouanne/	208
Maunoury	
12 Buthiers	224

DIRECTIONS

10 kms north of Etampes just east of the N20. From the forest it's best to take the D837 from Milly to Etampes then the N20 direction Paris. Come off at Etrechy and follow signs for Chamarande. Go through the village and the L turn for the carpark goes under the railway line, opposite a gate for the chateau grounds.

Follow a small path east from the corner of the carpark. The yellow starts to the L in the dry river bed. The rest start L of the path which is parallel to the railway line.

CHARACTER

Shady and slow drying but clean despite the tree cover. Good in summer. Despite the distance from the main climbing areas it's worth a visit.

CLIMBING

An excellent varied massif with something for everyone.

White (children's 50 problems)

Yellow PD- (62 problems) Good beginner's circuit. Well marked.

Orange AD (21 problems) Many intermediate boulders.

Blue D (40 problems) Good varied circuit. Mostly good landings.

Red A TD- (38 problems)

Red B TD (33 problems) Both reds are fingery and technical with some bad landings.

Black/White ED+ (37 problems) Sustained at a high level. Some bad landings.

There are also two easy circuits west of the carpark; a children's WHITE and a YELLOW.

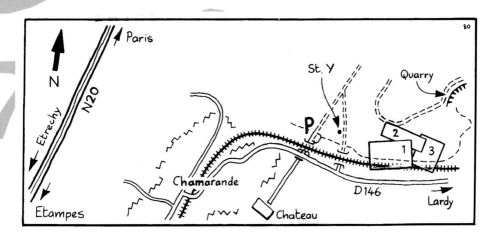

1   **1R 4-**   START Red A
2   **2R 4+**
3   **1B/W La Dalle P.O. 5+**
                START Black/White
4   2B/W Le Rayon Vert 6c
5   3R 5+
6   1bB 5-   1B 3+ to the L
                START Blue
7   **2B 3+**
8   **10 3-**   START Orange
9   **20 4-**
10   3B 3+
11   **4R Le Sémaphore 5**
12   5B 4
13   30 2
14   6B 3-
15   7B 3
16   8B 2+
17   5R 4-
18   **6R 4+**
19   **40 Le Cervin 3**
20   **3B/W L'Arête de Zmutt 5+** Rising Rward
    traverse.
21   **7R 5+**
22   **8R 5+**
23   **4B/W L'Abominable 6b**
24   9R 5
25   10R 4-
26   **5B/W Pousse Moussue 6a**
27   **6B/W Retour à la Terre 7a**
28   11R 5
29   **12R L'Angle Alex 4+**
30   **13R 4+**
31   14R 5
32   15R 4+
33   16R 4-
34   17R 5
35   18R 4+
36   19R 4-
37   20R 5+
38   21R 4
39   22R 4-
40   ?
41   60 2+
42   23R 5-
43   24R 4

44   25R 5+
45   **7B/W Le Portique 6b**
46   26R 5-
47   27R 4-
48   9B 4-
49   **10B Perverse Libellule 3+**
50   11B 4+
51   100 3-
52   210 2   END Orange
53   **12B Les Petits Câlins 4-**
        12bB Nathalia 5-
54   13B 3+
55   14B 4
56   15B 3 15bB 5
57   16B 4
58   17B 3+
59   18B 4+
60   19B 4-
61   20B 3+

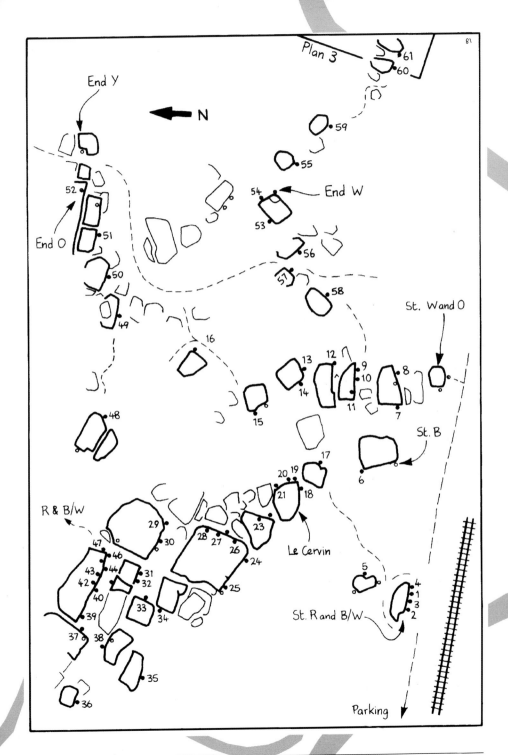

1	**8B/W Jinotega 6b**
2	28R 4-
3	29R 5-
4	30R 3+
5	**31R 4+**
6	32R 5+
7	33R 4
8	34R 3+
9	35R 4+
10	36R 4
11	37R 4+
12	9B/W Contact Mortel 6c
13	38R L'Empi de Gauche 4+
	END Red A
14	**33R L'Empi 4** END Red B
15	10B/W Résurgence 6a
16	32R 4-
17	31R 5-
18	11B/W Autopsie d'un Boeuf 6b
19	30R 5-
20	**29R 5+**
21	28R 5-
22	12B/W Quitte pour la Peur 6a
23	13B/W In Transit 6b
24	27R 4+
25	14B/W Pierre de Lune 6c
26	**26R 5+**
27	25R 4+
28	24R 4
29	23R 4+
30	22R 5-
31	21R 4+
32	**15B/W Ravage 7a**
33	**16B/W Visa USA 6b** R to L

34	20R 6a
35	17B/W Aborigène 5+
36	19R 5-
37	18R 4+
38	17R 5+
39	16R 4
40	18B/W Un Hiver de Clown 7b L to R
41	**19B/W Terre des Bêtes 6c**
	20B/W Combat de Rues 6c
42	15R 4+
43	14R 5
44	13R 4-
45	12R 5
46	11R 4+
47	bB/W? R to L
48	28B 3+
49	29B 3+
50	30B 3
51	31B 3+

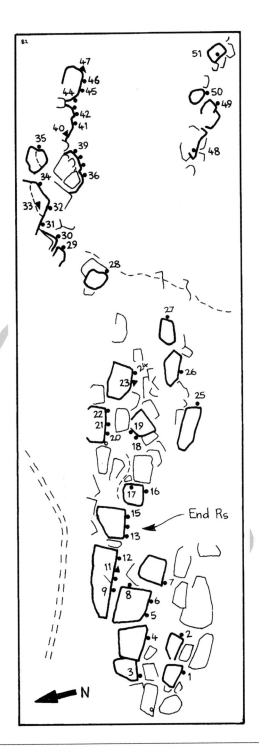

1	**1R La Cervelle 5**	START Red B
2	2R 5-	
3	**3R Docteur Excentric 5+**	
4	4R 6a	
5	5R 5+	
6	**6R La Dalle Icare 5-**	
7	**7R 5+**	
8	**8R L'Anti Renfougne 5**	
9	9R 5+	
10	10R 4	
11	**21B/W La Foire d'Empoigne 6b**	
12	22B/W Forêt Cruelle 7a	
13	23B/W Idées Noires 6b R to L	
14	24B/W SOS Amitié 5+	
15	**25B/W L'Empire du Soleil 6c**	
16	26B/W Sky Rock 6c	
17	27B/W Ma Nuit Bleue 6a	
18	**28B/W Joy 6c** R hand exit **7a+**	
19	29B/W Secrets de la Mer Rouge 6c	
20	**30B/W Dites-le avec le Rose 6b**	
21	31B/W Ton Dernier Trango 6a	
22	**32B/W Pierre de Thaï 6c**	
23	33B/W Tintin au Thibet 6a	
24	34B/W Neurone 6a Rising R to L	
25	35B/W Cortex 6b	
26	**36B/W Chamalo 6b** R to L	
27	37B/W Canicule 7a L to R	
	END Black/White	
28	21B 4-	
29	22B 3+	
30	23B 4	
31	24B 3	
32	25B 4	
33	26B 4+	
34	27B 3+	
35	32B 3+	
36	33B 3+	
37	34B 4	
38	**35B 3+**	
39	36B 4	
40	**37B 4**	
41	**38B 3-**	
42	39B 4-	
43	**40B 5-**	END Blue

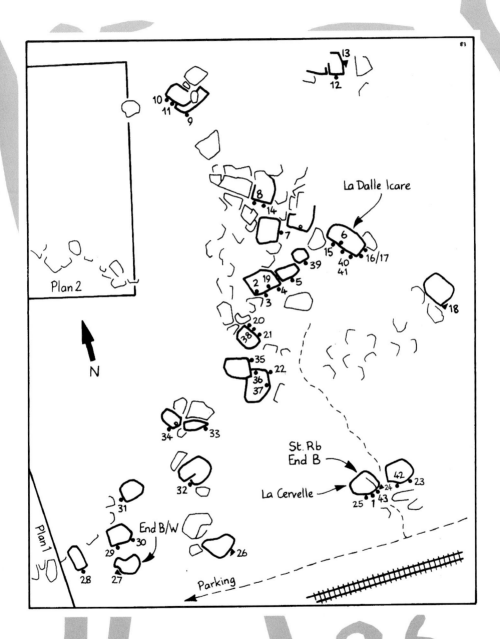

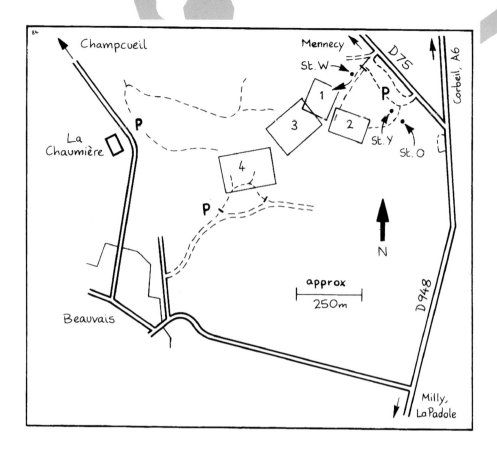

DIRECTIONS

For plans 1, 2 and 3 follow the D948 (between Milly-la-Forêt and Corbeil-Essonnes). Then take the D75 heading NW, direction Mennecy. Large car park almost immediately on your L.

From the car park take the path at its R (north) end. Shortly afterwards on the R is a particularly large tree. From here, cut off diagonally up to the R, working your way up and past various easy problems to find the start of the red and black/white circuits. Alternatively you can continue up the main path to the col for the start of plan 2, or from the col a short hike up the slope on the R takes you to the start of the blue circuit, and just beyond it, the start of plan 3.

For plan 4, take the road 1km south of the D75, direction Beauvais. Take the first on the right just before entering the village, then right again along a track. Park soon after, at the second barrier.

Follow the path that heads off to the left. At the fork you can head left or right; the problems begin soon after. 3 minutes from the car.

Another carpark is worth mentioning, although not as near to the good climbing, on the west side of the massif. Situated on the road between Beauvais and Loutteville, it's just in front of La Chaumière (see 'Where to eat' in the intro). There's a blue circuit that begins down and left of La Chaumière. Behind this, there are many orange and yellow problems. The blue works its way up rightwards to the crest of a ridge. Follow this ridge eastwards and you get to the large flat-topped boulder on plan 4.

CHARACTER

This is a complex massif, rarely visited by non-locals. This is a pity because the climbing, atmosphere and situation are superb. There's a fair amount of shade, although it can get fearsomely hot in summer. Dries quite slowly.

CLIMBING

White Children's
Yellow PD (45 problems)
Orange AD (45 problems)
Orange no.6 AD+ (41 problems)
Yellow (aka "Safran") AD (93 problems)
2 Blues no.8 D+ (38 problems) and no.1 D (50 problems)
Red TD+ (40 problems)
2 Black/White no.9 ED (41 problems) and no.15 ED+ (30 problems)

The climbing at Beauvais is superb. In general the boulders are low and the landings good. You will spend much of the time with your bum scraping along the ground as Beauvais is well known for its traverses – most are technical and strenuous, even the 'easy' ones.

1 **1R 5** R to L   START Red no. 4
2   46B 4
3   47B 4-
4   1B/W L'Eloge de la Différence 7a L to R
      START B/W no.15
5   2B/W Le Mouton Noir 6c
6   44B 4-
7   3B/W Sang d'Encre 6a
7b Le Gynécologue 7a
8   43B 4-
9   5B/W Le Grain de Beauté 6c L to R
10 **4B/W Coup de Blues 6c.** The superb L arete.
11 **4bB/W L'Etrave à Sucre 7b** Ride the R arete on pretty shoddy holds to an easier finish. Superb.
12   48B 4
13 **2R Le Coq Six 5+** R to L
14   49B 4-
15 **6B/W Bagdad Café 6a+** Neat little wall with a tricky start.
16   3R 5
17 **50B 4-**
     END Blue no. 1

18   7B/W Mathilde 7a+ R to L
     7bB/W 7b
19   1B 3-   1b 4-
20 **4R Soleil Cherche Futur 5+** L to R
21 **33R Roc Autopsie 5+** L to R
22   3B 4
23   6R 5-
24   2B 3+
25   5R 5

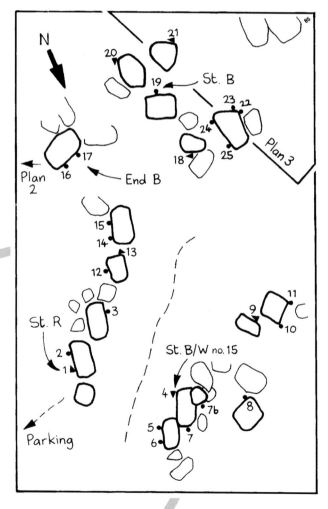

Either follow the path that leads from the R hand end of the carpark, passing the start of the children's white circuit on your R, to the top, where you'll find the first problem.

Or take the L hand path up past the start of the yellow and orange circuits.

1   34R 5   L to R
2   **22B/W Le Cambouis du Diéséliste 6c** R to L
3   Couple of good blues.
4   23B/W L'Amoco 6a L to R
5   24B/W L'Oeuvre au Noir 7a L to R
6   **24bB/W Le Dahlia Noir 7c** L to R
7   25B/W La Veuve du Fossoyeur 6b
8   26B/W Le Mâle Blanchi 6a R to L
9   37R 5
10 **36R Mauvais Sang 5+**
11 **30B/W L'Ebène 6b**

        END B/W no.15

30b La Perle de Jais 6c
30t Danse Macabre 7a L to R Starts to the L, exits R of 36R.

12 35R 6a
13 **29B/W Crawl en Mer Noire 6c** R to L
14 **27B/W Le Café Crème 6a**
15 38R 5
16 39R 5
17 **450**   END Orange
18 **28B/W Le Capuccino 6b**
19 **40R Tu ne Voleras Point 5**

        END Red

20 39bR 6a L to R

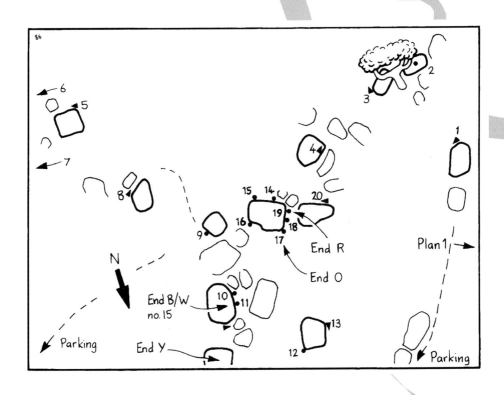

1 **7R Blatte Runner 6a** Nasty exit!
2 8R 5
3 8B 4
4 13B 3+
5 **8B/W Le Nègre en Chemise 7a+** L to R
6 9B 3
7 12B 4
8 **9B/W La Mouche 7a** Just to the R is 7b/7b+
9 10R 5 11B 3+
9a **Le Frigo 6b**
9b 10B/W Le Black-out 7a L to R 38B 4 L to R
10 11R 5
11 7B 3-
12 32R 5
13 **30R L'Ouvre Boîtes 6a**
14 5B 3+
15 6B 3-
16 **31R Néanderthal Roc 5+**
17 14B 4
18 12R 5
19 16B/W M & Ms 6b
20 **14R Le Boeuf Carotte 5+**
21 15B 5-
22 **13R Art Pariétal 5+**
23 Thug out of the cave and don't forget that heel hook! Finish direct **6c**, L **7a** or R **6a+.**
24 17B/W L'Anthracite 7a
25 35B 4-
26 **11B/W Les Abysses 6b**
27 **28B 4**
28 15R 5
29 **12B/W Le Petit Ramoneur 6b**
30 13B/W Les Ongles en Deuil 6c
31 24R 5+
32 29B 4
33 **23R Le Bonsaï 6a** L to R Short but thuggy.
34 16R 5+
35 30B 4-
36 17R 5+
37 **34B Le Long Fleuve Tranquile 4-** R to L 34b 4
38 19R 5
39 **18R Les Chaires Mobiles 5**
40 **20R J'ai Fantaisie 6a**

41 **33B 4-**
42 31B 4-
43 22R 5-
44 32B 4-
45 21R 5-
46 **14B/W Le Cliché N & B 6c+** R to L A fine test of power and technique. Burly types continue L **7b+.**
47 25R 5-
48 **15B/W La Magie Noire du Derviche 7a** L to R. Action packed traverse with a sting in the tail.
49 **26B 3+**
50 **18B/W Le Brou de Noix 6b**
51 22B 4-
52 26R 6a L to R
53 21B 3+
54 20B 4-
55 19B 4-
56 **18B 3+** L to R
57 17B 4
58 20B/W 6b
59 **28R Le Biodégradable 5+**
60 **19B/W L'Onyx 6b**
61 29R 5 R to L
62 21B/W La Dame Noire 6b L to R

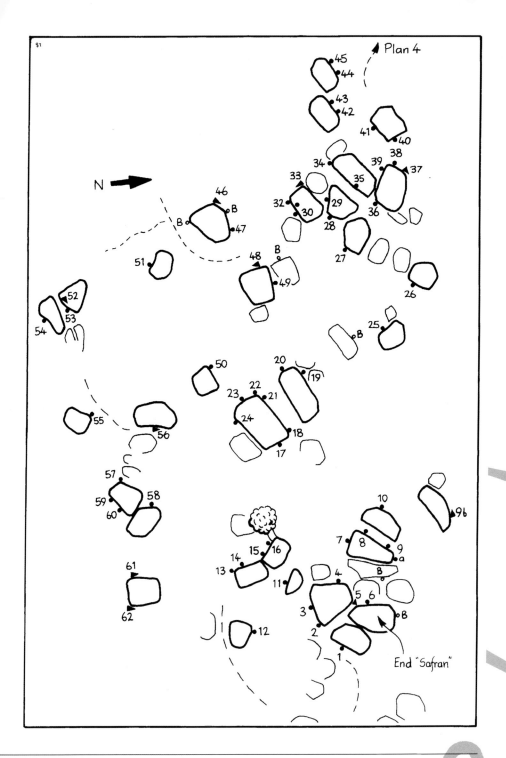

1	41B/W L'Epave 6b L to R	
	END B/W no 9	
2	10 4	START Orange no 6
3	**1 B/W Zest 6a** R to L	
	START B/W no 9	
4	20 3+	
5	2B/W Ex Abrupto 6a	
6	**70 3+**	
7	**3B/W Le Pavé Brulant 6a**	
8	4B/W Le Ras- pet 5+ L to R	
9	16B 5-	
10	5B/W L'Allée des Chevres 6a	
11	13B 4	
12	6B/W La Main Tendue 5+	
13	160 4-	
14	14B 5	
15	**8B/W Le Coup de Pouce 5**	
16	10B 4	
17	**11B 4+**	
18	10B/W Coup de Jus 6b	
19	12B 4+	
20	140 4-	
21	8B 4+	
22	11B/W Hérode 5+ L to R	
23	12B/W Petit Gibus 6a R to L	
24	110 3+ **Sale Histoire 7a R to L**	
25	**12bB/W Le Démonte Pneu 6c** L to R	
26	3B 4+	
27	5B 5-	
28	4B 4+	
29	16B 5+ Start on L	
30	1B 4	
31	15b B/W 6a	
32	15B/W Tribalite 6a	
33	28B/W Zébulon 6a	
	28b Le Steak à Chier 6a	
34	24B/W L'Entorse 5+	
35	21B 5-	
36	22B 5-	
37	**24B 4+**	
38	**27B/W Etat Dame 6a**	
39	25B 5	
40	33B/W Tout un Plat 6a	
41	26B 4-	
42	**21S 2-** Cracked slab.	
43	**21bS 3+** Steep juggy prow.	

44	32B/W Le Père Peinard 5-	
45	**27B 4**	
46	**36S 3**	
47	**29B/W Incarnadine 5+**	
48	28B 5-	
49	32S 3+	
50	30B/W Le Loup de Soir 5+	
51	29B 4+	
52	30B 5-	
53	31B/W En Catimini 5+ L to R	
54	33 B 4+	
55	34B/W La Chamoniarde... 6b	
56	32B 4-	
57	17S 3	
58	17bS 3+	
59	**16S 2**	
60	**35B/W L'Ivraie 6a**	
61	34B 5-	
62	**15S 3**	
63	36B/W Le Dragon de Vertus 6a	
64	**35B 5**	
65	**36B 4+**	
66	37B/W La Chamade 6a On the same boulder...	
	37b Le Mauvais Penchant 5	
	37t La Ballade du Vieux Faisan 7a L to R	
	and up.	
67	37B 4+	
68	38B 4+	END Blue
69	5S 3	
70	**38B/W Le Dernier Cri 6a**	
71	38bB/W Les Barettes 6a	
72	**39B/W Le Joug 6a** L to R	
73	**40B/W Le Bonnet Frigien 6a** R to L	
	40b L'Eté Indien 6c L to R	
74	1S 3- START Yellow "Safran" no. 5	

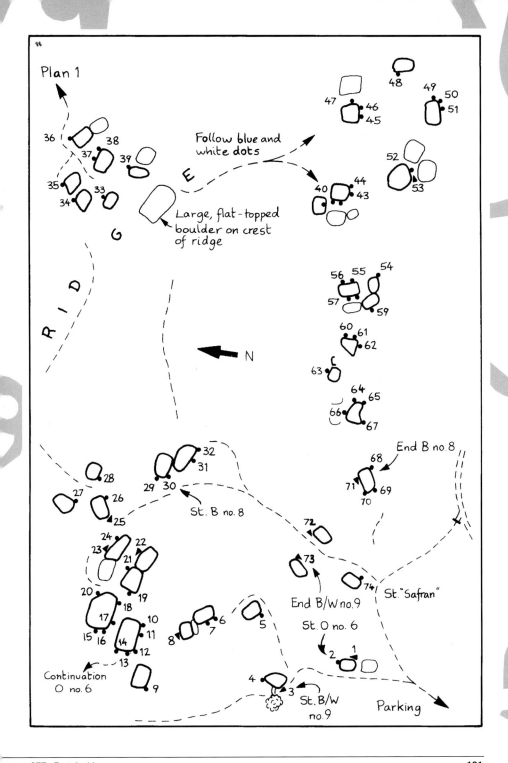

Plan 1

Follow blue and white dots

Large, flat-topped boulder on crest of ridge

R I D G E

N

End B no.8

St. B no.8

St. "Safran"

End B/W no.9

St. O no.6

Continuation O no.6

St. B/W no.9

Parking

LA PADOLE

DIRECTIONS

As for Beauvais, follow the D948. Then take the D83, direction La Ferté-Alais. After about 300m a track cuts off diagonally to the right, towards the woods. Follow this, passing a barrier on the left and a small building on the right, and park on the right, in one of 3 small places on the edge of the woods (the 3rd is best). Just to the left of the third space take a small path up into the woods, bearing left. You're looking for a little craglet about 6/8 ms high. This is the Locomotive. Problem 1, plan 1 is just to its right.

CHARACTER

A strange little massif, where you can almost guarantee peace and quiet. Pixies and other small folk are often sighted here (BETA unreliable). Some parts of the massif are very enclosed and overgrown, (although most of the problems are clean), and tend to dry slowly. The highlight of the Padole however, the chaos of boulders on plan 1, dries fairly quickly. A good spot in summer BUT LOOK OUT FOR VIPERS.

CLIMBING

Yellow PD (33 problems)
Orange AD (53 problems)
2 Blues no. 2 D+/TD- (35 problems) and no. 6 D (25 problems)
2 Reds no. 1 TD+ (30 problems) and no. 5 TD (27 problems)
Black/White ED+ (38 problems)

There is a good selection of really superb climbing here and although good landings do exist, some of the problems, especially on the Locomotive and in the chaos of boulders above it, are hard and bold, combining commiting climbing with bone crunching landings. Except for the Locomotive, most of the more trouser-filling problems have big, juicy bolts cemented in at the top. So BRING A ROPE!

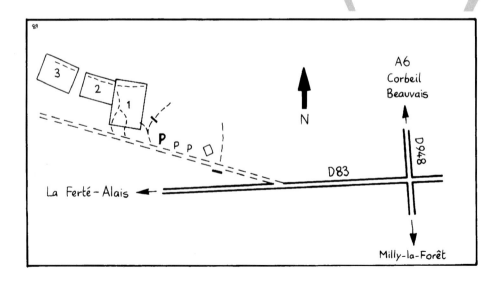

Eric Letot on La Dernière
Croisade 6c, La Padôle.
Alain Hoffman

1   1R La Forfaiture 5   START Red no. 1
2   8 B/W La Calobra 6b
3   1B L'Alphabète 4   START Blue no.2
4   2B Médecine 5
5   9 B/W Odeur de Vestiaire 6b
6   2R Toboggan 4-
7   3B Dalle au Clou 3+

The following nine problems are on the Locomotive; a craglet where a rope may be useful...

8   4B L'Angle Obtus 4+
9 6B/W Carte Orange 7b. The bold bulging wall, past bolts.
10   5B/W La Vie du Rail 7a
11 5B Le Cheminot 5- The unusual (for Bleau) groove.
12   3R Les Bavures Jaunes 4+
13   4B/W T.G.V. 6b
14   4R 5+
15   5R Fissure de Tender 5
16   6B Lanterne Rouge 4
17   1Y 2-   START Yellow
18   7B 4
19   5B 5-
20   3Y 2
21   4O 2+
22   2B/W Chocolat-pistache 5
23   1B/W Pastels 6b   START B/W
24   3B/W Le Croazou 6c
25   6R Carmagnole 4 Up and R, past the jugs, and up to finish.

Many of the following problems have got bolts at the top.
26   12R La N.O. du Sandwich 4+
27   30B 3+
28   9R 5+
29   8R 5+
30   31B 3
31   10R La Gitane 6a
32   10B/W Anti-takat 6a
33   11R 5+
34   32B Mur de Son 4
35   11B/W Le Temple Maudit 7a
36   29B La Dalle Verte 4

37   28B 4-
38   Mechoui 7a
39   Kani-Basami 7a+ L to R from 40 to exit up 43
40   12B/W Les Aventuriers 6b
41   13R Salle à Manger 5.
42   14R L'Echo-muet 5
43   13B/W La Dernière Croisade 6c
44   14B/W Sabbah 6b At least one variant to the L; 7a+/7b
45   33B 3+

The next four problems are being rapidly reclaimed by Mother Nature...
46   6a
47   6b
48   6c (sitting start)
49   7a
50   16B/W La Cache 6b
51   15B/W Svobodu 6a
52   15R Enfin Heureux 5. Excellent L-slanting groove
53   Tsubame-Gaeshi 7b L to R. Start at 52 Finish up R arete.
54   17B/W L'Ami Bernard 6c
55   18B/W Bagdad Café 6c
56   16R Le Bivouac 5
57   35B La Chevauchée Héroïque4+ Rising R-ward traverse   END Blue no. 2
58   17R Lime à Ongle 5
59   18R Service Compris 5+
60   19B/W Tien Anmen 6a

Start in the bowels of the earth for the next 4 problems and have a good spotter...
61   Do-Jime 7b Start from the ground
62   Yama-Arachi 7a+
63   Tani-Otochi 7a
64   19R Bande d'Urgence 5+ Bleausards find this crack desperate. Gritstoners will love it.
65   20R L'Expo 36 5+
66   20B/W Tombé du Ciel 6a
67   21B/W Alertez les Bébés 6b

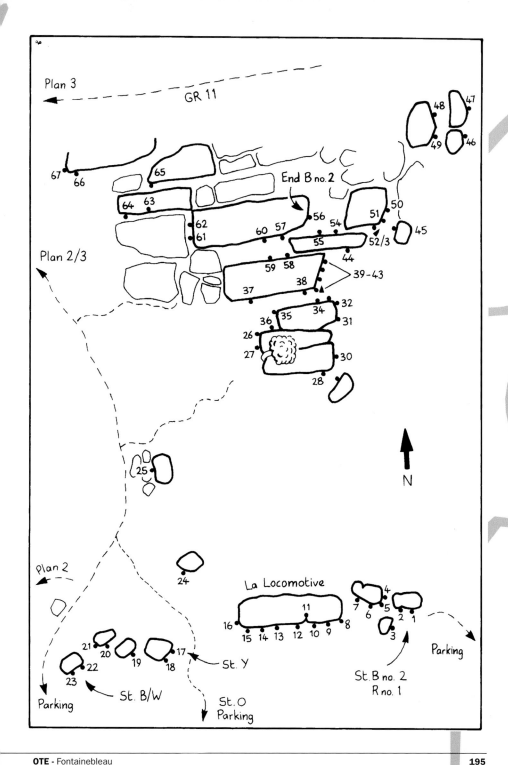

1 26B 4+
2 22B/W Le Désert sans Lumière 6a
3 25B 4+
4 23R L'Equivoque 5+
5 24B Drapeau Noir 4
6 23B Vote Secret 5-
7 25R Ciel, Beau comme Moi 6b
8 27R Feuilles Rousses 5
        END Red no.1
9 24B/W Blues Brothers 5+
10 23B/W Les Yeux de Fer Rouge 6c
11 26R Miette d'Amour 5+
From 11, bear L and descend to...

12 19B 4
13 110 3
14 13B 4+/6a
15 26B/W Pictionary 5+
16 27B/W Bye bye Eighties 6a/b
17 25B/W La Dame de Berlin 7a+
18 130 2
19 14B 4+
20 28B/W Le Voyage à Cythère 6a
21 17B 5-
22 16B 4+
23 15B 3+

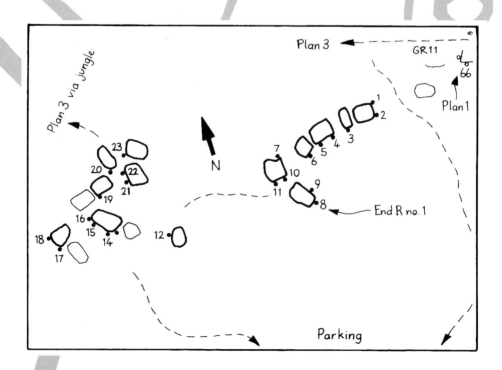

Philippe le Denmat on Plein Gaz
4+, Rocher Gréau.
Alain Hoffman

1	19B 3+	
2	26R 4+	
3	20B 4	
4	21B 4+	
5	29R 5	
6	37B/W Le Petit Ecolier 6b And further to the L...	
	38B/W Guet-Apens 6b	END B/W
7	24B 4 Further to the L	END B
8	23B 4-	
9	22B 3+	
10	8R 5+	
11	10B 3+	
12	7R 5-	
13	330 3	
	Fin de Journée 7c L to R from 13 to exit up 20.	
14	13B 4+	
15	12B 4	
16	11B 4-	
17	**11R Paroles 4+**	
18	**10R Le Mandarin 5-**	
19	**9R Le Feu 5** R to L from red dot on 17, finishing up 14.	
20	**33B/W Kango 6b/c**	
21	**32B/W Délice Choc7a**	
22	370 3+	
23	9B 4-	
24	5R 4+	
25	**30B/W Cookie Break 6b**	
26	**16R Le Planétarium 4+**	
27	15R 4	
28	**31B/W Kalimantan 6b**	
29	14R 5	
30	13R 4+	
31	12R 5	
32	14B 4-	
33	**34B/W Semeuse Camée 6a**	
34	490 3	
35	15B 4	
36	**16B 3+**	
37	17R 4+	
38	**18R Le Pain Dur 5+**	
39	25R 6a	
40	24R 5+	
41	23R 5	
42	18B 4+	
43	**410 3-**	
44	22R 4+	
45	17B 4-	
46	400 4-	
47	7B 4-	
48	6B 4+	
49	5B 3+	
50	4R 5-	
51	4B 4-	
52	2B 4	
53	2R 5-	
54	3B 3+	
55	1R 4+	START Red no. 5
56	1B 4-	START Blue no. 6

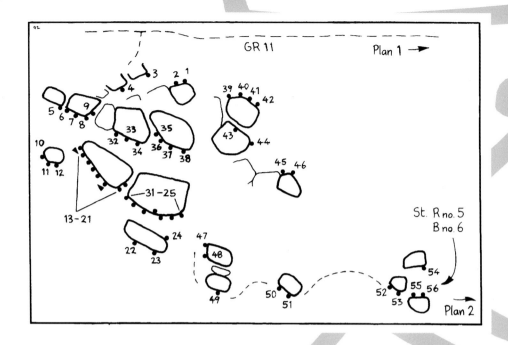

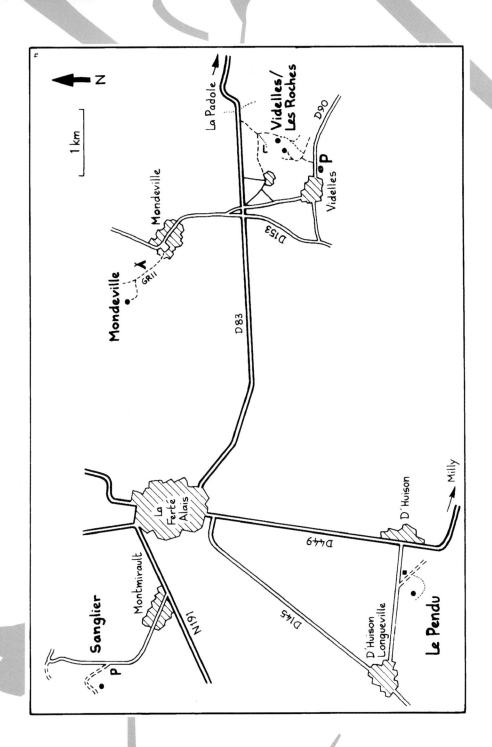

N

1 km

La Padole →

Videlles/
Les Roches

D90

Mondeville

Mondeville

D153

Videlles

P

Mondeville

GR11

D83

Milly →

D'Huison

La Ferté
Alais

D449

Sanglier

Montmirault

D145

D'Huison
Longueville

Le Pendu

N191

P

MONDEVILLE
DIRECTIONS
4 kms east of La Ferté-Alais. As for Videlles/Les Roches but continue straight on and turn R onto the D153 direction Mondeville. Park in the square in the centre of the village. From its corner follow the GR11 west for about 1 km, passing a caravan park on the R. Soon after this the GR11 turns L. Follow it to a chaos of boulders just below the edge of the plateau. The problems start here.

CHARACTER
Quiet and slow drying. Rather dirty in parts but pleasant in summer.

CLIMBING
Orange
Blue
Red
Black Starts near the end of the red
Deserves more attention. Some superb problems and some appalling landings.

VIDELLES/LES ROCHES
DIRECTIONS
7 kms east of La Ferté-Alais. From Milly take the D948 then the D83 direction La Ferté-Alais. Turn L direction Videlles. Once in the village turn L and park near a pond at the exit to the village on the R. A little after the pond on the other side of the road is a track leading towards the woods. Follow it. Where the track meets the woods either turn R and immediately L and follow a path up onto the plateau. You're looking for a small quarried bay just L of the path where the pink, blue, red and black/white circuits start. Or turn L and follow the path round to the R into the woods, keeping R at a fork. The orange and yellow circuits start just L of the path.

CHARACTER
A quiet and very complex massif which is totally bewildering on first aquantaince. Slow drying.

CLIMBING
Yellow
Orange
Blue
Pink D-
Blue D+
Red TD (61 problems)
Black/white ED (48 problems)
Many fine problems at all levels although this area has more than its share of atrocious landings. The red and black/white circuits finish in a small quarry to the NW of the massif. Most of the problems are in the confusing chaos of boulders just below the plateau.

LE SANGLIER
DIRECTIONS
2.5 kms NW of La Ferté-Alais just north of the village of Montmirault. Approaching from La Ferté-Alais take the D N191 direction Etampes. At Montmirault turn R and once through the village follow the road through some fields. Soon after it goes into the woods a small stoney track cuts up L, just before a clearing on the R. Park just before the track on the L. Walk up the track. The circuits start over to the L before the track reaches the top.

CHARACTER
Very quiet and slow drying. Pleasant in summer.

CLIMBING
Yellow PD- (40 problems)
Orange AD (28 problems)
Red TD- (28 problems)
Not destined for great popularity, this massif nevertheless has some good climbing. A rope may be useful for beginners on some problems.

LE PENDU
DIRECTIONS
Situated 3.5 kms south of La Ferté-Alais, between D'Huison and D'Huison Longueville. From Milly take the D105 then the D449 direction Le Ferté-Alais. At D'Huison turn L direction

D'Huison Longueville. There's a garage on the L at 500m. Turn L down a track and park discreetly. The path goes into the woods beside a pile of stones. Follow it up the hill and the circuit starts near the top off to the R, hidden away at the foot of the remarkable Roche Cornue.

CHARACTER
Quiet and quick drying. There have been access problems here so best behaviour please. Climbing is tolerated if visitors are small in number and quiet.

CLIMBING
Blue D+ (27 problems) A classic, varied and constantly interesting with a fine finish.
There are a number of arrowed harder problems.

ROCHER GREAU
DIRECTIONS

Just outside (south west) of Nemours. Take the D403. Go up a hill and then turn R at some lights, direction St-Pierre-les-Nemours. Take the first on the L and park in front of the Town hall. The problems start on the other side of the road, just after entering the park.

For le Petit Bois continue straight on for another km until the road becomes a track and park next to the trees by a R hand bend. The rocks are up to the L.

CHARACTER

Slow drying and quiet.

CLIMBING

Some of the forest's finest problems but with a few exceptions, they're mostly hard and highish. There are no circuits at Rocher Gréau but several are under way at le Petit Bois.

LE PETIT BOIS

This area has been extensively brushed and the marking of circuits is underway. There already exists two superb problems. As you go into the woods from the parking space they're up to the R on an obvious pocketed wall. Top roping bolts in place.

Big Jim 6c The L hand weakness.
Passage à l'Acte 7a Just to the R.

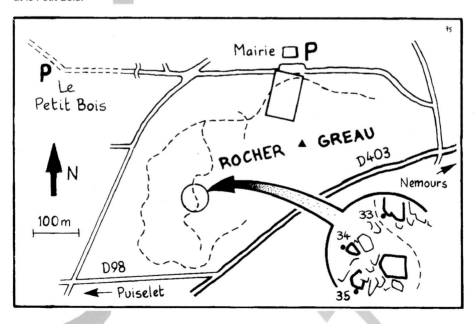

1 Entrée en Matière 5+ (without arete)
2 Les Feux de le Rampe 6a (exit L by big crack)
3 La Pyramide 6b (without ramp exit by vertical crack)
4 Chauffe Marcel 5+
5 Rapelle toi Minette 6c
5a Droit d'Option 5+ direct 6a
6 Le Pitbull 6b Bold. Exit by hole.
7 Le Dernier Cri 6c Top rope
8 La Tour Infernale 6c Top rope
9 Plein Gaz 4+
10 L'Abbé Réta 6b Start by undercuts
11 R to L traverse?
12 Un Monde de Brutes 6b Without big holds on R.
12a Oliver Twist 7a+
13 **Le Jeu t'es Fou 7a** Exit by central arete.
14 La Consolation 6b
15 Choucroute Système 5+ The crack.
16 Le Dièdre 5+
17 Mégalithe 7b+/7c Climbs L side of big prow. Exit R arete.
18 Les Conquistadores 7b Straight up the middle. Exit L arete.
19 La Cocotte Minute 6a
20 Médecine Douce 5+
21 Caprice des Lieux 6b
22 Le Pied de Nez 6c Start good hold R hand
23 Le Rince Doigts 6a
24 Faux Fuyants 7b
25 Serre Moi la Pince 6a

26 Little Big Boss 6b 7b from back.
27 La Directe des Poires 6c
La Traversée des Poires 6b, goes R at mid height to exit on good holds.
28 Patience Yago 7a Bold.
29 Le Flamand Rose 6a
30 L'Arête Meurtrière 6a Top rope.
31 Balade Sentimentale 5 With arete.
32 Gros Bourin 6c Start from bloc

The remaining 3 problems are marked on the access map on the previous page...
33 Direct 5, R finish 6b
34 3 problems L 6b, arete 6a, R 6a
35 Plein Vol 7c+ The steep slab has 3 methods. Once stood at the top of the ramplet either; finish direct 7c+ with a horrendous fingernail rockover, or L 7a, or using R arete 7b. Only the direct has been done without a rope.

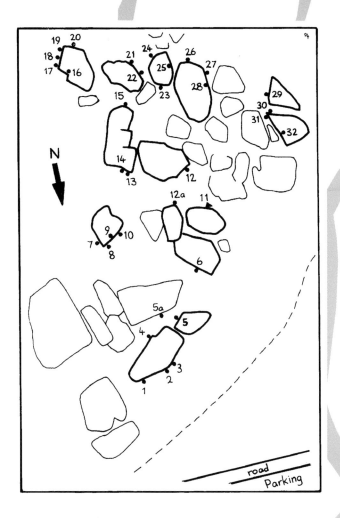

DIRECTIONS

4 kms west of Nemours, which can be reached by the A6 or the N7 from the north. From Nemours take the D16 direction Larchant and turn L for the village of Puiselet. Just after a R hand bend, at the bottom of a hill, turn R and follow a track trending L to parking spaces next to a sandpit/tip.

CHARACTER

Dead quiet. The south side of the ridge dries fast. The rest stays slimey for some time after rain. It is becoming very dirty in parts, especially the north side, although cleaning of the black circuit is under way.

CLIMBING

Orange AD (19 problems) Traces a loop, working its way over to the adjacent pignon before returning to the main massif.

Black ED (33 problems) This classic circuit has fallen into neglect, partly because of its location but also because many of the problems are approaching Himalayan proportions with horrendous landings to boot! Still interested? Bring a rope. The scariest micro-routes have huge bolts cemented in at the top. A lot of brilliant climbing which doesn't deserve its obscure status.

SE of this massif, on the other side of the road is Sablibum, a mixture of quarried and natural rock. Some impressive 'last great problem' type features (especially the arete in the east bay) and some potential for bouldering and micro-routing. Cavers have peppered much of it with bolts. There's an 8a bolted line up the steep wall in the west bay.

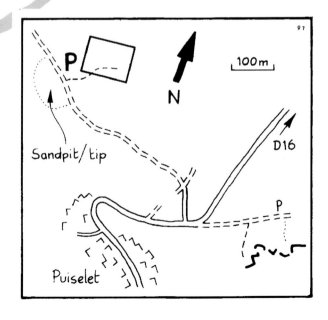

The black circuit.

1 Novembre 5+
2 Alubiade 5
3 Archipel 6a
4 Arcanson 5+   4b L'Echapée 5
5 Chrysalide 6b
6 Le roc à billy 5+
7 Mandragore 5+
8 Cosmetik 6a
9 Eldorado 5
10 Torticolis 5
11 Mathusalem 6c 11b L'Enfer Vert 4+
12 Sangora 5
13 L'Idiome 5
13a, 13b and 13c all 6c and flipping high!
14 Le Champignon Magique 5
15 Myriade 6a
16 Minerve 5+

17 Le Palimpeste 5
18 Chemin de la Postérité 6b
19 Fissure des Forçats 5-
20 Ballade pour un Matin 5-
21 Remise de Peine 6c
22 Ketchup 5
23 Fissure des Soupirs 5-
24 Sérénité 5-
25 Cardiac Blues 6b
26 Gaelique 5
27 Paul et Mick 5-
28 La Moustik 5-
29 Tonien 5+
30 L'Ombilic des Limbes 5
31 Mystères 6a
32 Vingt Mille Lieux sous les Mers 6b
33 Exuberance 5

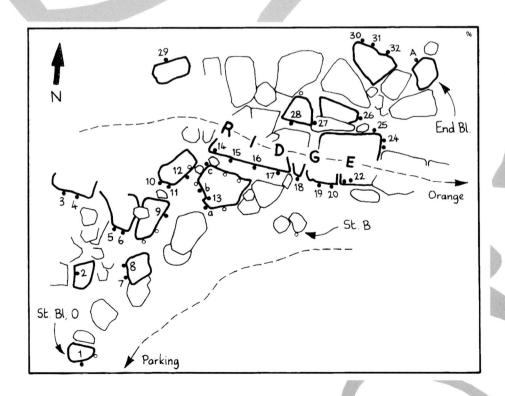

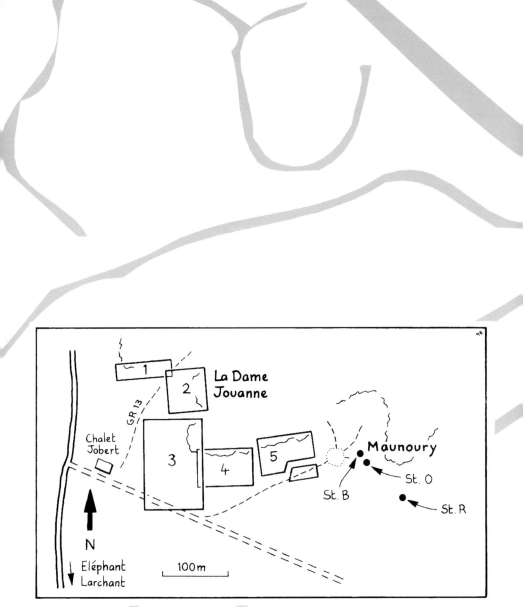

La Dame Jouanne

1

2

GR 13

Chalet Jobert

3

4

5

Maunoury

St. O

St. B

St. R

N

Eléphant Larchant

100 m

DIRECTIONS

La Dame Jouanne

2 kms north of Larchant which can be approached via la Chapelle-la-Reine from Milly or Nemours from the east. Once in the village La Dame Jouanne is signposted. Turn R and park near the Chalet Jobert.

Maunoury

As for La Dame Jouanne as far as the car park. Walk along the track and pass the start of the DJ red no.3 (plan 3). Then take a path that cuts off obliquely L to skirt the foot of the slope. This eventually brings you to a sandy clearing. Cross it trending slightly R. You're looking for a tall slim boulder with the start and finish of the blue circuit. The orange starts a little higher to the R. The start of the red is well hidden at the foot of the south side of the pignon.

CHARACTER

La Dame Jouanne

Attracts hordes of tourists. Erosion is a big problem here and steps will probably be taken in the future to try and limit its spread. Dries fairly quickly but treat the rock with care. It can be friable, especially after rain. Hot in summer.

Maunoury

Very hot in summer. Dries fast. Quiet.

CLIMBING

La Dame Jouanne

The first two circuits are similar in style, tracing enormous, vaguely parallel loops around the massif. Countless arrowed but unnumbered intermediate boulders. Some of the mauves are magnificent but if you don't have a rope YOU MUST NOT FALL OFF! The Bleau equivalent to a day out in the mountains. Woolly socks, thermos and box of sarnies de rigueur!

Yellow PD (110ish problems)
Mauve AD+ (76 problems)
Blue D (47 problems)
Red no 3 TD- (58 problems)
Red no 5 TD-/TD (48 problems) Like the red no 3, excellent varied climbing.
Red no 8 TD+/ED- Epic and unfinished.

Problems range from 5+ to 6c and are arrowed with red dots to distinguish them from other reds. Some good problems and many minor variants and traverses. Some of them are marked on the plans as R..

White ED (31 problems) Classic. You need strength, technique and at times, courage.

Black "alphabet" circuit ED+ A to Z. Recent gap plugger but some excellent gaps. Not all problems had been lettered at time of writing, in which case they're listed as Bl.

Maunoury

Orange PD+ (54 problems)
Blue D- (71 problems)
Red TD (36 problems)
Overshadowed by its neighbour but a lot of fine climbing. Quite a lot of bold problems, despite the often sandy landings.

1	**1R Les Trois Trous 4+**	
		START Red no. 5
2	**2R Bloc Agée5**	
3	**3R Castor à Moi 5-**	
4	**4R Castor direct5**	
5	5R 5-	
6	6R 4	
7	7R 4+	
8	8R 4+	
9	9R 5-	
10	10R 5-	
11	Bl A 6b/c	START "alphabet"
12	**11R Plaquage 5-**	
13	12R 5-	
14	**13R 5+** R to L	
15	14R 5-	
16	15R Mini Dur 5 Just L Aspranax 7b/c	
17	1R..	START Red no. 8
18	**16R 4+**	
19	17R 5	
20	Bl D Balladium 6c/7a R to L	
21	**Bl B Moselle 6b**	
22	**Bl C Vertibloc 6b/c**	
23	18R 4+	
24	19R 5-	
25	20R 5	
26	21R 5-	
27	22R 5-	
28	Bl E Epmé Noir 6b	
29	Bl F Cachalot 7a R to L	
30	**71M 3+**	
31	3 good 5s here.	
32	23R 5-	
33	24R 5	
34	**Bl G Scolopendre 7b/c** L to R or R to L (return 8a) Finish (or start) on ramp of 36.	
35	R.. From back of 'cave'.	
36	**68M La Dalle du Feu 3** Rising Lward traverse.	
37	**25R Trous Durite 5**	
38	Bl H L'Heure H 6c/7a	
39	**26R 6a** L to R	
40	27R 4	
41	28R 4	
42	**2W Le Grand Noir 6a**	
43	29R 4+	
44	30R 5-	

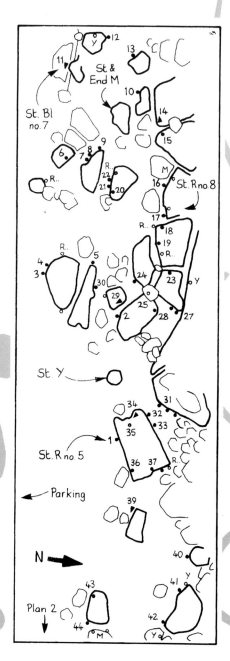

1	31R 5-		15	**41R Pour quelques Betteraves! 6b** R to L
2	32R 5-		16	42R 5+ R toL
3	33R 4+		17	6W Le Trou Normand 6b
4	34R 4+		18	7W Le Trou de Secours 6a
5	35R 5-		**19**	**8W Extractor 6c** L to R
6	36R 4+		20	43R 5-
7	**1W Le Pied Là 6b** START White		21	44R 5-
8	3W Le Toit du Koala 6b		22	45R 4+
9	4W Culbutor 6c		23	46R
10	37R 5		24	47R5-
11	38R 5		**25**	**48R 5** END Red no. 5
12	5W La Dalle Verte 5		**26**	**9W La Rampe 5+**
13	39R 4		**27**	**10W La Gouttière 5+**
14	40R 4+			

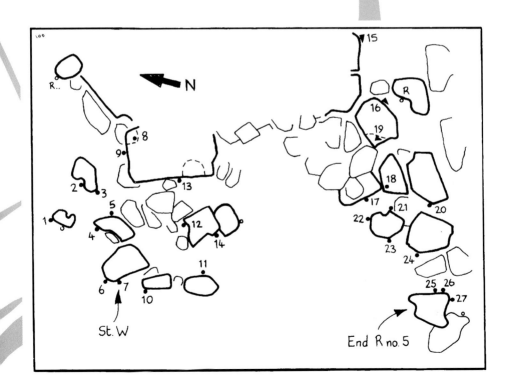

1	1R 4+	START Red no. 3
2	47B 4	END Blue
3	2R 4+	
4	3R 5	
5	Bl Mur Mur 6c	
6	4R 4+	
7	5R 4	
8	40B 4-	
9	14W Spélman 6b	
10	17W L'Angle Mort 5	
11	32R 4+	

12 33R L'Abri à Bras 5-
Bl Le Plafond 7b/c Start at back R side of cave

13	7B 4+
14	34R 4-
15	10B 4
16	35R 5-
17	36R 4+
18	37R 4+
19	38R 5-

And on la Dame Jouanne herself...

20 52M L'Arête de Larchant 4

There are other micro-routes here, most harder and deserving a rope.

21 39R 5+ R to L traverse

22 24B 5-

23 Bl Imitation Promenade 7a Long R to L traverse. Beware dodgy rock.

24 23B 3+

25 40R 4+ (without arete)

26 Bl Monument Dalle 7a

27 41R 4+

28 42R 5-

29 11W L'Ours Blanc 6a L to R and up

30 19B 3+

31 57M 3+

32 44R 4+

33 18B 3+

34 13B 4-

35 15B 5-

36 45R 5-

37 47R 4+

38 48R 5

39 Bl La Boule 7b/c R to L

40 12W Le Tendu 6b   46R 4-

41	49R 5-	
42	**13W Le Trou de l'Anord 6c**	
43	**50R 5-**	
44	1B 4-	START Blue
45	Bl Nuage 7b/c R to L	
46	Bl Etoiles 7b R to L	
47	2B 4-	
48	51R 5-	
49	52R 5-	
50	53R 4+	
51	54R 5	
52	5B 4-	
53	55R 4	
54	44B 4-	
55	56R 4+	
56	43B 4	
57	15W Le Dernier Empereur 6c	
58	42B 4-	
59	57R 4+	
60	41B 4	
61	16W Sans l'Angle 5+	
62	58R 5-	END Red no. 3

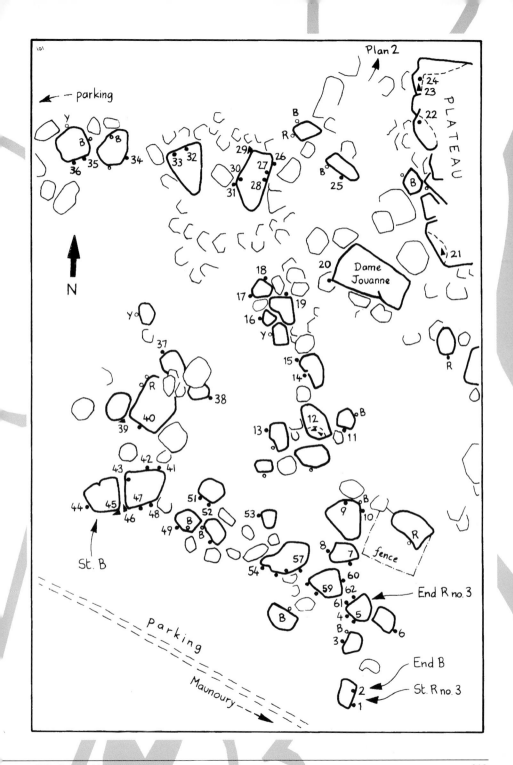

1 7R 5
2 18W Le Pontet Bas 6a+ R to L (aka De Marbre)
3 8R 4
4 9R 5
5 10R 5-
6 11R 5-
7 12R 4-
8 13R 4-
9 14R 4+
10 15R 5-
11 19W L'Expo Supo 6b
12 20W Le Bras Carré 6b
13 16R 5-
14 17R 4+
15 18R 5
16 21W Predator 7a
17 Excellent faint groove 7a?
18 19R 4+
19 20R 4+

20 39M 2+
21 21R 4
22 28M No. 1 de la Dalle aux Pigeons 3+
23 Chair et Cuir 7a+ Chipped but superb moves.
24 22W Le Pied Main 6a
25 23R 5-
26 23W L'Angle Parfait 7a+ Some very strong folk fail on this beautiful problem. A winter at the wall helps not at all. Some say it's the best of its grade in the forest.
27 24R 5-
28 29B 4
29 25R 5
30 28B 3+
31 27B 4
32 33B 4
33 41M 3-
34 71Y
35 26R 5 L to R

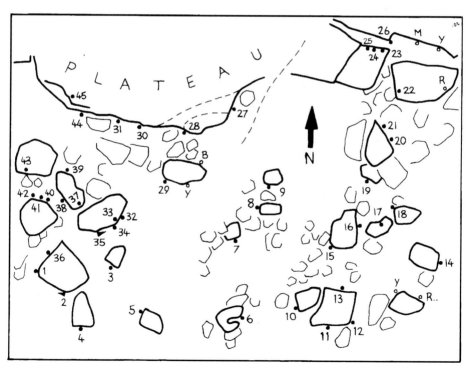

36	45M 4-	**5**	**34M 3**
37	42M 2	6	35M 3
38	35B 4	7	Bl U Choux Bloc 7a
39	29R 4	8	10 START Orange
40	**43M 3**	9	26W Anse Lazio 6c
41	La Roullette Russe 7a (top rope)	10	Bl V Bonne Amie Bonne Sauté 7b/c
42	30R 4	**11**	**27W Les Grottes de Kocamador 6a**
43	**36B 4**	**12**	**28W L'Ecaille Cassé 6a**
44	27R 4+	13	29W Le Surbac Plomb 6b
45	28R 4+1	**14**	**30W Tetehamor 6a**

R to L, up and back.

15 31W La Crampe à Rachid 6b R to L
END White

La Dame Jouanne plan 5

1	31M 4-
2	**24W Les P'tits Plats 5+**
3	**Bl T Anti-G 7a/b**
4	**25W La Tranchante 6a**

16	Bl W La Grenouillère 6c/7a	
17	Bl X Arrêt sur Image 6b/c	
18	**Bl Y Stretchin 6c+/7a**	R to L
19	Bl Z Devertige 7a	END "alphabet"

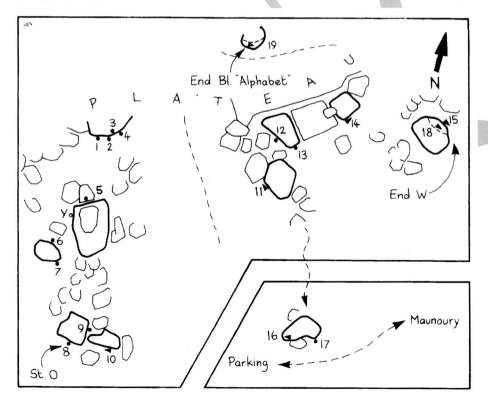

DIRECTIONS

About a kilometre north of Larchant, which is best reached via the D16. If you're on the A6 come off at Nemours or Ury. Once in the village follow signs for la Dame Jouanne. There's parking on both sides of the road, near a ruined building with a fountain on the R, about 750m out of the village.

CHARACTER

Very popular, attracting a lot of foreign climbers as well as coach loads of tourists. Can get very hot, particularly on the quick drying southern flank. Treat the rock with care, especially after rain when it can be rather brittle. Even the most solid looking holds have been known to explode! The terrain is very sandy which increases erosion problems and means the grades of many problems tend to fluctuate.

CLIMBING

White The first children's circuit at Bleau. Well marked and fun.

Yellow PD (49 problems) A beginner's circuit. Well marked. Most of it is found on the plateau.

Orange AD (44 problems) A classic; old fashioned (intermediate boulders) and difficult to follow but some outstanding climbs. Follows the edge of the plateau clockwise.

Blue D (84 problems) Very long and difficult to follow. The northern part is quiet. Varied, technical climbing.

Red TD- More or less abandoned, this exploits the eastern flank of the plateau and contains some impressive, sometimes bold problems. Of note; the no 61 and adjacent problems (see map).

Black ED (40 problems) A classic. Strenuous, high and bold at times, this circuit has some of Bleau's finest. Relatively finger friendly for a hard circuit.

ELEPHANT WEST

The end of the black circuit is a good spot to warm up for the following problems which are high for the most part, and hard. Slow drying but cool in hot weather.

Follow the GR13 from behind and R of the end of the black circuit until you see the 1st problems on an obvious large boulder on the R.

1	Elephant Man 6c
2	Super Tanker 5
3	La Gonflée 6b
4	**Le Grand Toit 6b+**
5	**Pas de Panique 6b**
6	La Muraille de Chine 5+
7	La Chamoniarde 5+
8	La Retraite Anticipée 5+
9	Saut de Puce 5+
10	Surprise sur Prise 6a
11	La Rampataplan 6a
12	La Désuète 5
13	Le Lézard 6b
14	Les Nerfs à Vif 7a+
15	Le Spectre 7a
16	Décollage Immédiat 5
17	L'Amuse Doigts 6c
18	La Détente Rapide 6c+

And the most impressive problems hereabouts....

19 Haut de Forme 7b
20 Coeur de Lion 7a
21 L'Aileron de Requin 7a

Another isolated spot but nearer the carpark is le Bout du Monde. Follow the Route de Blomont les Roches from the first parking spaces, keeping straight on where it turns R and turn L just before a small brick construction on the L. At the end of this smaller path you'll find:

Bout de Monde 6c+ A pumpy R to L (or L to R 7a+, who cares!?) traverse along the lip from low on the R. If it's too easy try the return which pushes the grade up to 7blip or thereabouts.

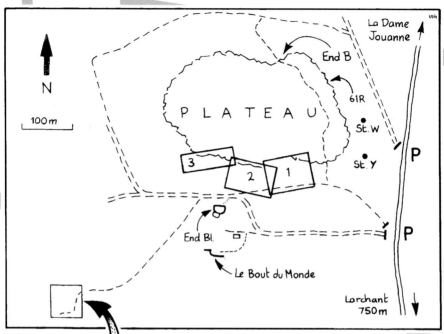

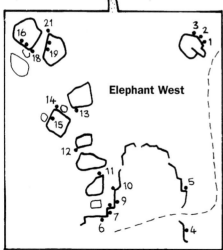

Elephant West

And on the eastern flank of the plateau, just L of an excellent slanting crack (61R) there are three good problems. From R to L...

Visage de Marbre 7b
Just R of corridor **6c.**
Just L of corridor **Coquine Bleause 7a.**

A little further north is the very hard looking **Mirobol**, with a proposed grade of 7c/8a and apparently, evolving holds. It's R of the 280.

1	**1G 4**	START Green
2	1R	START Red
3	1B 3+	START Blue
4	**1Bl 6a**	START Black
5	**2Bl L'Y 5+**	
6	**440**	END Orange
7	2G 4	
8	420	
9	**3Bl La Chute du Moral 6a**	
10	430	
11	10	START Orange
12	2B 4+	
13	3B 4	
14	4Bl 5+	
15	**5Bl 5+**	
16	**3G 5**	
17	4B 3	
18	4G 5	
19	**5G 5** Down and R to L.	
20	6G 3	
21	5B 3+ 5bB 5	
22	7G 4	
23	The overhanging wall exits L or R **7a+/7b.**	
24	6Bl 5+	
25	7Bl 5+	
26	7bBl 5	
27	**8Bl Le Mur de la Mort 5+** It will be if you fall off!	
28	**Le Pilier Droyer 6c** If you follow the edge of the plateau round to the R (east) from here you will find, 2m R of the 40 orange a very bold slab **J'Osais Fine 7b+**	
29	**La Figure du Proue 7a** The fine arete is normally gained by a delicate traverse from the R. Can be done direct.	
30	8G 3+	
31	7B Mur Lepiney 3+	
32	5	
33	6B 4	
34	8B 2+	
35	40	
36	9B 4	
37	9Bl 5	
38	10B 4	
39	14G 4	
40	13B 3	

41	**15bB 6b** Or leap to jug from adjacent boulder. Also here... La Traversée de la Barre Fixe 6c+ Start from pocket on the L and finish up 41.	
42	**15B 4+**	
43	10Bl Le Lancer 6b	
44	**18G 6b**	
45	19G 5	
46	16bB 5-	
47	**11Bl L'Appui 5+**	
48	**20G 5** Down crack (from 19G), R to L	
49	**17B L'Aigle Déployé 4+**	
50	**12Bl La Directe de l'Aigle Déployé 5+**	
51	21G 6a R to L and up	
52	13Bl 6a	
53	**14Bl 6c**	
54	**15Bl 5** Just R of the arete is la Claque 6c.	
55	**18B 4**	
56	19B 4+	
57	20B 3+ R to L	

Plan 2

1 21B 3
2 16Bl Le Médaillon 5
3 30G 5   END Green
4 17Bl Les 400 Buts 6b
5 29G 5-
6 18Bl Le Trou du Trio 5
7 19Bl 6b
8 22B 3+
9 23B 4
10 20Bl 6a
11 21Bl 6a **Le Lépreux 7a** L to R from 21Bl exiting up 20Bl
12 24B 3
13 25B 3+
14 26B 4+
15 22Bl 6c
16 23Bl 6a Also here **Monsieur Plus 7b+** R to L Finish up 18
17 26G 6a
18 24Bl 5
19 27B 3+
20 28B 4
21 25Bl 5
22 42B 4+
23 26Bl Le Bouton 6c
24 44B 4
25 43B 4+
26 25G 3
27 46B 5-
28 27Bl 5+
28a Protection Raprochée 6c
29 47B 4
30 48B 3
31 90
32 28Bl 6a
33 29Bl 5+
34 40B 3
Etat d'Urgence 7b+ is a top rope problem which takes the weakness in the roof.
35 30Bl 5+
36 70
37 39B 4-
38 40bB 5

39 La Traversée des Anges 6c (aka la Traversée des Dieux) L to R Athletic climbing on good holds with a spikey landing. Exit up 41
40 31Bl Le Toit du Loup 6b
41 23G 4+
42 32Bl Voie du Flirt 6c/7a
43 32B 4-
44 30B 3+
45 31B 4-
46 33Bl Le Pilier Légendaire 6c Wall to the R without arete is Haut de Gamme 7a+
47 Partenaire Particulier 8a Looks magnificent. Not been repeated for donkey's years. Most will need a stone to start. Top roping bolt in place.
48 33B 4-
49 35B 3+
49a Le Diagonal 7a+ Rising Lward line.
50 34Bl Le Mur aux Stères 5+   34bBl 6b
51 36B 4+ Direct 5 Left 4
52 37B 3+
53 38B 4+
54 35Bl 5
55 49B 4
56 51B 4

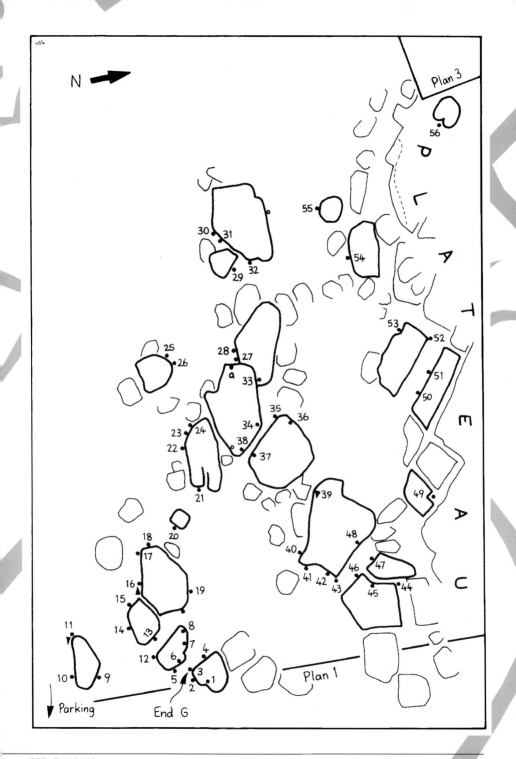

1   52B 3+

2   53B 4+ **53bB 5**

3   49Y   END Yellow

4   54B 3

5   55B 4

6   Le Coeur 7a Love at first sight! You will want to touch that hold but passing it is not easy.

7   56B 4-

8   36Bl La Directe du Rateau 6c

9   57B 4+

10 58B 3

11 59B 4-

12 60B 4

13 Envie d'Ailes 7b+ Excellent powerful problem on a gently overhanging wall. Several methods but the start is harder for the short.

14 61B 4+

15 Envie d'Air 7b L to R

16 120 62B 4+

17 37Bl 5

18 130

19 38Bl 6b

20 63B 5-

21 140

22 39Bl 6c

23 64B 4+

The blue and orange circuits continue clockwise round the edge of the plateau from here. Slow drying and dirty in parts but some fine problems and always quiet.

For the end of the black circuit walk south from le Coeur (no.6) for about 100m, crossing a couple of paths, before arriving at the remarkable Dalle à Poly, a hefty overhanging wall covered in pockets.

40Bl 5+ R to L and up   END Black

R to L low all the way is **6b 4+** direct to the highest point of the boulder. One of the forest's great pleasures. Steep but easy on perfect holds.

Also here...

Furibond 6c Climb out of hole at L side of bloc to join the 40Bl near the top. Low R to L + Furibond = 7c

---

DIRECTIONS

Just NE of Malesherbes, about 20kms south of Milly. From Fontainebleau take the N152 via Ury. From Milly or the Trois Pignons take the D410. At the bottom of a hill and before arriving in Malesherbes turn L at some lights following signs for la Base de Loisirs de Buthiers. Parking soon after, on the L first for the Canard massif (next to the auberge) and a little further turn R for the main carparks.

For the Massif de l'I (Piscine) pass the entrance to the swimming pool on your R. The circuits start soon after, next to the crazy golf.

CHARACTER

Can be very quiet at weekends although you may be overrun by millions of screaming school children in the week. The swimming pool (also full of screaming kids unfortunately) is a life saver - in summer at least. Both massifs dry fairly quickly

CLIMBING

A lot of brilliant climbing at all levels. Both massifs have more than their fair share of high problems and appalling landings, especially in the harder circuits, which is probably why they're so unfashionable.

Massif Canard
White (children's)
Yellow PD- (29 problems)
Orange AD (34 problems)
Blue no1 D+ (43 problems)
Black no4 ED (22 problems)
Massif de l'I (Piscine)
Orange AD- (44 problems)
Blue no2 D+ (42 problems)
Red TD+ (35 problems)
Black no3 ED (39 problems)

Buthiers has the dubious distinction of having some of the worst examples of chipped, drilled or sica holds in this guide. Le Roi du Pétrole, a traverse next to the start of the children's circuit, is apparently very popular, though it's hard to imagine why. Several classics seem to have been spared.

1 **La Mygale 7b+** Beautiful L to R traverse, vertical to start, then dropping down to a thuggy finish. As an alternative you can finish up the overhanging wall: Nouvelles Pauvres 8a. The wall is a good problem in its own right; **Le Mepris 7b**
2 **Dernier Bal 7b/c** L to R traverse
3 **7a/7a+** Nifty overhanging wall. Exit L or R.
4 **Coccinnelle 7c+** Classic traverse, normally L to R. 8a with return.
5 **Flagrant Désir 7c** The big white wall is bold and climbed direct. Very few repeats.
6 **Attention Chef d'Oeuvre 7a** The steep wall is magnificent!

1   **1BI Fissure Martin 6a**   START Black
   The wall to the R is 7a.
2   1B 4-   START Blue
3   2B 4
4   **2BI La Fissure des J3 7a**
5   3B 4
6   3BI La Dalle Noire 5+
7   **4BI Dalle Ultra 6c** Smear up the 'holdless'
   slab.
8   4O 4-
9   5O 3+
10   5BI Départ des Anciens Con Battus 6b
11   6BI A Bras Carrés 6c
12   17B 3+
13   20B 4
14   22B 3+
15   21B 3
16   16BI Rire de Battardive 5+
17   17BI Les Séchelles 6b
18   32O 3
19   31O 4-
20   19B 3+
21   **18BI Angle de la Galotte 6a**

22   23B 3+
23   19BI Musclor 7a
24   25B 4-
25   24B 4
26   26B 4+
27   Les Yeux de l'Esprit 7c Roof/traverse.
28   27B 3+
29   28B 4
30   **29B 4**
31   30B 4
32   31B 4
And two bold problems....
33   **20BI Bouledogue Direct 6a**
34   **21BI L'Angle du Bouledogue 6c** The arete
     is magnificent and very dangerous...or
     back and foot up the tree.

End of Black and Blue circuits about 75 m
east.
22BI L'Etoffe des Zéros 6b
                   END Black
43B 4+   END Blue

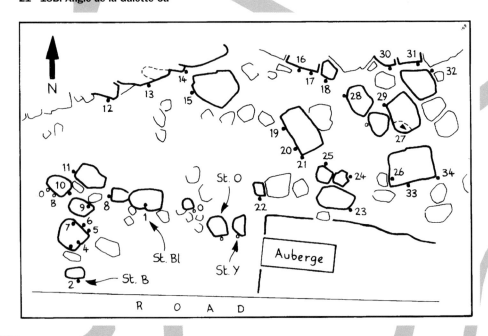

1 70 3
2 4B 4-
3 5B 4
4 6B 4-
5 7B 3+
6 8B 4
7 80 3+
8 9B 4
9 90 3-
10 10B 4
11 230 4
12 13B 4
13 210 2+
14 14B 3+

15 **9Bl Lopo Table 6a**
16 120 4-
17 **Petite Sirène 7a+** L to R
18 160 4-
19 10Bl Mystère Klein 5
20 **11Bl Angle des Soviets 5-**
21 12Bl Rage de Nains Géants 6c
22 13Bl Squeletor 6b
23 **14Bl Mur Droyer 6c+** Fairly awesome, rarely climbed and stiffly graded.
24 15Bl Fissure Rose 6a

For the end of the Black circuit, see plan 1.

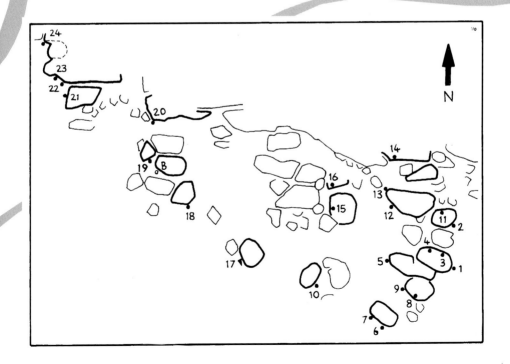

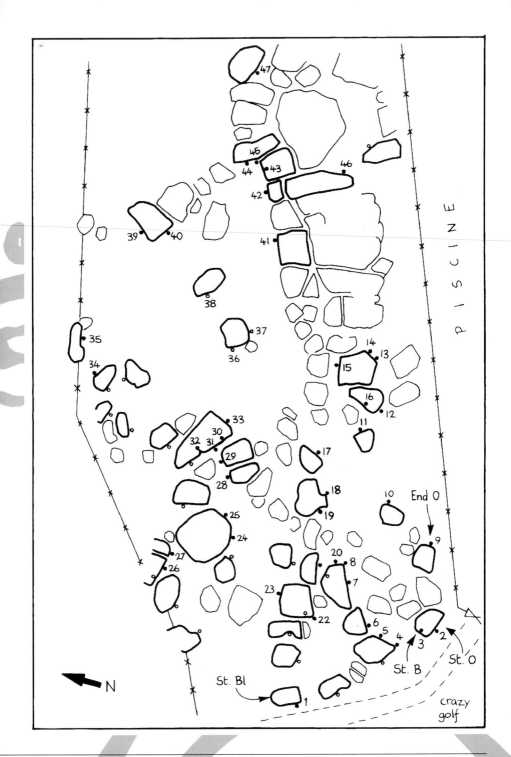

1   28B 3+
2   12Bl La Descheneaux 5+
3   29B 4+
4   30B 4
5   13Bl 5+
6   31B 3
7   32B 4+
8   33B 3
9   34B 4
10 14Bl La Voie Lactée 6a
11 15Bl L'Excuse 6b
12 16Bl Le Cource Doigt 6c
13 1R Le Sphinx 6b   START Red
14 **7b** R to L Exit up 13
15 17Bl Le Perlin Pinpin 5+
16 R L to R
17 36B 5
18 18Bl La Yano 5+
19 5R L'Astatigne 4+
20 37B Le Teinaret 4-
21 **38B 3+**
22 6R L'Usi 5+
23 **39B La Fissure de l'I 5-**
24 **19Bl La Duchesse 6b** Just L is a bold 7c.
25 40B La Fissure Verte 5-
26 **20Bl La Voie Mercier 6c**
    Master Edge 7b Arete L of 26
27 **Misanthropie 8a** Ferocious crimpfest
    which has had few, if any, repeats.
28 21Bl 5+
29 22Bl La Brutus 6a
30 **42B La Fissure Brutus 4+**   END BLUE
31 41B Le Minaret 4+
32 7R 5
33 **23Bl La Traversée du Culot 6b**
34 8R 5-
35 24Bl La Dynamostatique 5+
35b **Le Flipper 6c+**
36 9R 5-
37 11R 5
38 12R 5+
39 **25Bl L'Etrave 6a**
40 **26Bl L'Angle de la Fresque 5+**
41 **27Bl La Super Fresque 6c**
42 13R La Fresque 5-
43 28Bl L'Ultra Son 6b

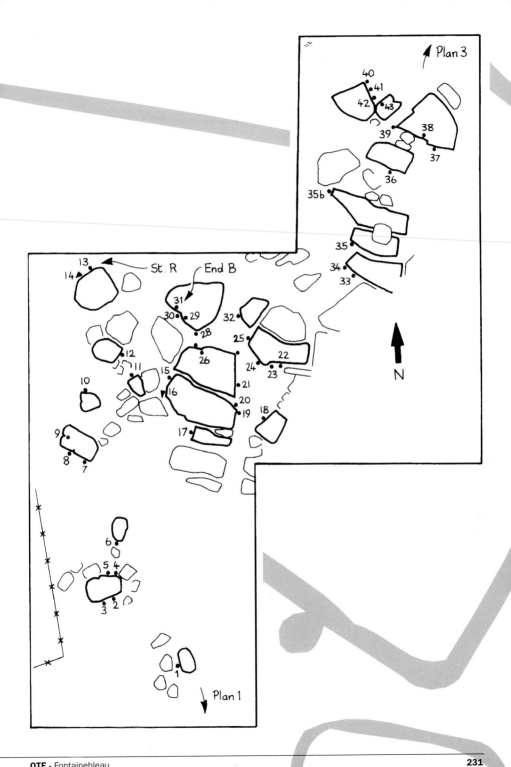

1   29Bl La Coupe Rose 5+
2   16R 5
3   30Bl Le Surplomb Taillé du Pique Nique 6c
4   20R 6a
5   31Bl La Dalle Poulenard 5+
6   22R 6a
7   32Bl Le Surplomb de l'Usi 5+
8   33Bl 5
9   34Bl 5
10   35Bl Le Charleston 6a
11   31R 5+
12   Le Strapal 7a
13   36Bl Le Swing Medium 6b
14   24R 5
15   25R 5+
16   26R 5
17   28R 6a
18   33R 5+   Just L is Platre et Ciment 7b+
19   37Bl Rêve de Singe 6b
20   38Bl L'Allumeuse 5+
21   34R 5
22   39Bl La Réfractaire Directe 5+
          END Black
23   35R 5   END Red

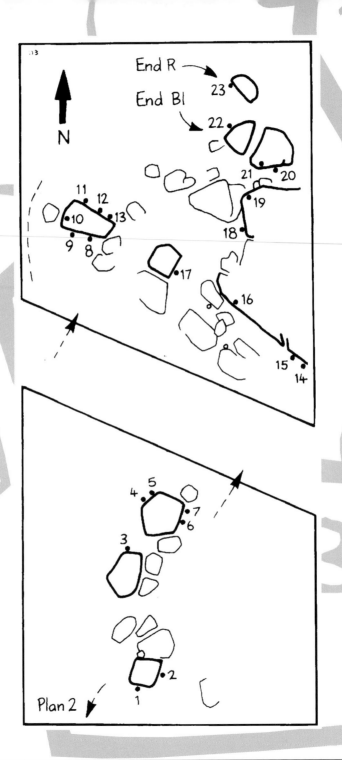

The following, extremely subjective list of some of the forest's outstanding climbs, was compiled from the views of the following climbers: Philippe le Denmat, Jo Montchaussé, Jacky Godoffe, Stéphan Denys, Severine le Menestrel, Baptiste Briand, Pascal Terray, Alain Thibault, Jean-Pierre Bouvier, Bernard Theret, Jean-Denys Darigol, Benoît Faure, Marc Boulard, Catherine Micquel, Olivier Carrière, Christophe Laumone, Michel Libert, Robert Paragot, Olivier Penel, Dany Riche, Didier Gerardin, Damien Boitard, Christophe Bougon, David Rastouil, Caroline Morel and last but not least, Big Frank Lemoine. MERCI BEAUCOUP A VOUS TOUS!

Asked to make a list of their favourite problems their choices were dictated by three main criteria: the beauty of the boulder, technical interest and in some cases, a desire to publicise their own obscure and rarely climbed problems!

Most of them found it difficult to come up with anything easier than 5+. Apologies then to lower level climbers for the high level bias in this list. But don't be put off. There are millions of brilliant problems between 2 and 4 in the forest!

Just for interest's sake, four problems came up time and time again:

La Liberté 6b,
le Toit du Cul de Chien 6c/7a,
le Mur des Lamentations 7b/7b+
Rubis sur l'Ongle 7b+.

Have fun!

2 TO 3

Apremont
190 no. 1 Les Verrues (plan 5)
Gros Sablons
730 no. 1 Les Trous du Gruyère (plan 3)

3 TO 4

Bas Cuvier
500 La Prestat (plan 2)
Le Pendu
27B L'Arête de la Ferté
Gros Sablons
400 no. 2
10 no. 1
Eléphant
1G Le Trompe de l'Eléphant (plan 1)
420 (plan 1)
8G (plan 1)
La Dame Jouanne
53M L'Arête de Larchant (plan 3)
68M La Dalle du Feu (plan 1)
Apremont
200 no. 1 Le Paquet (plan 5)

4+ TO 5

La Padole
13R Salle à Manger (plan 1)
Rocher Canon
6LB L'Attrappe Mouche (plan 3)
Bas Cuvier
20B La Borniol (insert 2)
48B La Paillon Directe (plan 2)
27R Le Quartier d'Orange (plan 2)
Apremont
31bLB Le Surplomb de l'Avocat (plan 5)
Cuisinière
4W Le Hareng Saur (plan 1)
Isatis
9B (problem 45 plan 1)
95.2
35W (plan 3)
Long Rocher
22R Le Pascalien
Rocher Gréau
Plein Gaz
Eléphant

40Bl La Dalle à Poly (direct up the middle)
La Dame Jouanne
1R no.5 Les Trois Trous (plan 1)
Malesherbes
39B La Fissure de l'I (plan 2 Piscine)

5+

Mondeville
69R Envie de Lumière
Bas Cuvier
22Bl La Digitale (aka la Fissure du Crocodile)
(plan 3)
Cuvier Rempart
Angle Allain (plan 2)
Apremont
7LB Le Gibbon (plan 3)
25LB La Vie Lente (plan 6)
34R no 12 La Science Friction (plan 5)
46R no 12 Le John Gill (plan 6)
Cuisinière
5W (plan 1)
20W (plan 2)
Isatis
15W Le Statique (plan 1)
16W Le Coup de Pompe (plan 1)
95.2
1W Kilo de Beurre (plan 3)
Gros Sablons
2Bl La Mandarine (plan 1)
4Bl La Piscine (plan 1)
12Bl La Brosse à Dents (plan 1)
14Bl Gueule d'Enfer (plan 2)
Roche aux Sabots
1R (plan 3)
22R (plan 2)
28R (plan 2)
Rocher Fin
2R

6A

Bas Cuvier
22R La Marie Rose (insert 2)
8Bl Erectissima (plan 2)
16Bl La Brioche (plan 3)
Apremont
28R no 12 La Conque (plan 6)

24S La Balafre (plan 5)
11R no 12 Les Yeux (plan 5)
Isatis
Beurre Marga (plan 1)
Le Bois Rond
22R Le Meilleur des Mondes (plan 2)
Gros Sablons
22Bl L'Everest (plan 2)
95.2
7W(plan 2)
10W (plan 2)
25W (plan 1)
91.1
12R (plan 2)
Cul de Chien
6R La Nano
7R
JA Martin
4R La Coquille (plan 2)
La Dame Jouanne
2W Le Grand Noir (plan 1)
Malesherbes
1Bl no.4 La Fissure Martin (plan 1 Canard)
20Bl no. 4 La fissure du Bouledogue (plan 1 Canard)
3Bl no. 3 Surplomb de Marbre (plan 1 Piscine)
25Bl L'Etrave (plan 2 Piscine)

6B

Bas Cuvier
15W La Stalingrad (plan 2)
La Padole
1B/W Pastels (plan 1)
14B/W Sabbah (plan 1)
Isatis
18W L'Envie des Bêtes (plan 1)
W La Planquée (plan 2)
Gros Sablons
35bBl La Liberté (plan 3)
JA Martin
1R (plan 2)
Elephant
14Bl (plan 1)
31Bl Le Toit du Loup (plan 2)
Buthiers
19Bl La Duchesse (plan 2 piscine)

6C TO 6C+

Beauvais
4B/W no 15 Coup de Blues (plan 1)
Calvaire
Le Toit de Calvaire
Bas Cuvier
1W La Lili (plan 1)
6W La Défroquée (insert 1)
22bBl Le Bivouac (plan 3)
29Bl Duroxmanie (plan 3)
Apremont
9W Le 13ème Travail d'Hércule (plan 5)
Roche aux Sabots
17bR (plan 1)
Rocher Gréau
La Directe des Poires
Eléphant
33Bl Le Pilier Légendaire (plan 2)
22Bl (plan 2)
Buthiers
4Bl Dalle Ultra (plan 1 Canard)
14Bl Mur Droyer (plan 1 Canard)
21Bl L'Angle du Bouledogue (plan 1 Canard)
Le Flipper (plan 2 piscine)

6C+/7A

La Padôle
13B/W La Dernière Croisade (plan 1)
Bas Cuvier
Charcuterie (insert 1)
Apremont
1W Hyper Plomb (plan 5)
Isatis
48cW El Poussah (plan 3)
95.2
Pierre Précieuse (plan 1)
Cul de Chien
Le Toit du Cul de Chien

7A TO 7A+

Rocher Canon
Chasseur de Prises (plan 3)
Bas Cuvier
Holey-Moley (insert 1)
Le Biceps Mou (insert 1)
L'Araignée (insert 1)

5W La Boucherie (insert 1)
6bW Abbatoir (insert 1)
13W La Joker (insert 2)
La Super Forge (insert 2)
La Merveille
Le Sourire de David
Apremont
2bW Médaille en Chocolat (plan 5)
Fleur de Rhum (plan 5)
Cuisinière
L'Innomé (plan 3)
3BI Excalibur (plan 4)
5BI Descente aux Enfers (plan 4)
33BI La Teigne (plan 4)
95.2
32W Le Mur de la Fosse aux Ourses (plan 3)
29bW Mister Proper (plan 3)
Roche aux Sabots
24bR A l'Impossible Nul n'est Tenu (plan 2)
Eléphant
8bBI La Figure de Proue (plan 1)
Le Coeur (plan 3)
Dame Jouanne
23BI L'Angle Parfait (plan 4)
Monument Dalle (plan 3)
Buthiers
2BI Fissure des J3 (plan 1 Canard)
Unnamed (problem 3, Buthiers map)

7B TO 7B+
Beauvais
4bB/W Etrave à Sucre (plan 1)
Bas Cuvier
Fluide Magnetique (plan 1)
4bW L'Angle Incarné (insert 1)
6tW Carnage (insert 1)
17W Super Prestat (plan 2)
Pince mi Pince moi (insert 1)
29bBI Michel Ange (plan 3)
Cuvier Rempart
Big Boss (plan 1)
Apremont
Une Idée en l'Air (plan 3)
Isatis
12bW Le Mur des Lamentations (plan 1)
52bW La Memel (plan 4)

La Canche
Rage dedans (plan 2)
Roche aux Sabots
15bR Lucifer (plan 1)
Cul de Chien
Le Toit aux Grattons
L'Autre Toit
JA Martin
L'Etrave (plan 1)
Les Béorlots
In Extremis
Gorge aux Chats
Rubis sur L'Ongle
Rocher Gréau
Les Conquistadors
Dame Jouanne
Le Plafond (plan 3)
Eléphant
Etat d'Urgence (plan 2)
Envie d'Ailes (plan 3)
Buthiers
Master Edge (plan 2 piscine)

7C TO 7C+
Bas Cuvier
La Bérezina (insert 1)
La Balance (insert 1)
Hypothèse (insert 1)
L'Ange Gardien (plan 2)
Digitale (insert 2)
Cuvier Rempart
Fourmis Rouges (plan 1)
Tristesse (plan 1)
Big Golden (plan 1)
T. Rex (plan 1)
Apremont
Jolie Môme (plan 2)
Isatis
Gnossienne (plan 1)
Gymnopédie (plan 1)
La Super Joker (plan 1)
Alta (plan 3)
Le Bois Rond
Lucky Luke (plan 1)
95.2
L'Ange Naïf (plan 3)

Roche aux Sabots
Déviation (plan 1)
Sale Gosse (plan 3)
Rocher Gréau
Mégalithe
Plein Vol
Buthiers
Flagrant Désir

7C+/8A
St Germain
Mégalithe
95.2
Futurs Barbares (plan 1)

8A TO 8A+
Cuvier Rempart
C'Etait Demain (plan 2)
Calvaire
L'Aplat du Gain
Cuisinière
Karma (plan 1)
Duel (plan 4)
Hale Bopp (Franchard map)
Cul de Chien
Integral of L'Autre Toit
Vallée de la Mée
Le Surplomb (plan 3)
Eléphant
Partenaire Particulier (plan 2)
Buthiers
Misanthropie (plan 2 piscine)

8B
Apremont
L'Alchimiste (plan 6)

"Traverse grades are meaningless." Jacky Godoffe, the man who graded a fair number of the following. Some of the harder ones have had few, if any repeats.

5+
Beauvais
33R Roc Autopsie (plan 1)

6A
Beauvais
23R Le Bonsaï (plan 3)
Bas Cuvier
Les Crampes à Messner (plan 2)
Apremont
7R no.12 Les Crampes à Mémère (plan 5)
Isatis
Wb (plan 3)
Long Rocher
3R Elixir de Bouldering

6B
Beauvais
29B/W Crawl en Mer Noire (plan 2)
Rocher Greau
La Traversée des Poires
Dame Jouanne
18W Le Pontet Bas (aka De Marbre) (plan 4)

6C TO 6C+
Beauvais
14B/W Le Cliché N &B (plan 3)
Rocher Canon
L'Académicienne
Bas Cuvier
La Longue Marche (insert 2)
Eléphant
Bout du Monde
La Traversée des Anges (plan 2)

7A TO 7A+
Beauvais
7B/W Mathilde (plan 3)
8B/W La Nègre en Chemise (plan 3)
15B/W La Magie Noire du Derviche (plan 3)

Rocher Canon
Miracle
La Levitation (plan 2)
Bas Cuvier
Kilo de Beurre (insert 2)
Le Bois Rond
21bR Tour du Bloc (plan 2)
La Canche
Ni Vieux ni Bête
Roche aux Sabots
Le Tourniquet (plan 3)
Buthiers
Petite Sirene (plan 1)

7B TO 7B+
Rocher Guichot
Jardin Secret (Trois Pignons south map)
Rocher Canon
Vagabonde des Limbes (plan 2)
Trois Graines d'Etenité
Bas Cuvier
Banlieue Nord (insert 2)
Expo en Ciel (traversée du bivouac plan 3)
St Germain
Danse de Printemps
Cuisinière
Eclipse (plan 1)
Isatis
L'Intégrale (plan 1)
Roche aux Sabots
Parti de Jambes en l'Air (plan 3)
Eléphant
Monsieur Plus (plan 2)
Buthiers
La Mygale

7C TO 7C+
St Germain
Les Yeux plus Gros que le Ventre
La Vie Devant Soi
Bas Cuvier
Bérézina/Carnage (insert 1)
Cuvier Rempart
Massacre au Supermarché (plan 1)
La Minute Nécessaire de Monsieur Cyclopède

(plan 2)
La Canche
Soléa
La Longue Marche (plan 2)
Roche aux Sabots
Miss World (plan 1)
La Dame Jouanne
Scolopendre (plan 1)

7C+/8A
Bas Cuvier
Les Pieds Nickés (plan 3)
Isatis
Mystification (plan 1)
La Canche
La Colonne Durutti
Buthiers
La Coccinelle

8A TO 8A+
Bas Cuvier
Sina qua non (plan 3)
Cuisinière
Liaisons Futiles (plan 1)
Isatis
Pierres en Pleurs (plan 1)

8B
Rocher Canon
Valse aux Adieux (plan 3)
Bas Cuvier
Le Mouvement Perpétuel (insert 1)

ESOTERICA

All these problem have the following characteristics in common:

They're off the beaten track or well hidden, they're not part of any circuit and they're totally excellent! The first two probably qualify for micro route status...

Inaccessible Absolu 7c top rope (Mont Aigu etc map)

Toutes Peines Confondues 7c top rope (Franchard map)

Voltane 8a Traverse near Isatis (Franchard map)

Le Surplomb de la Coquille 6c Isatis (Franchard map)

Petit Tome 7b Traverse near Franchard (Mont Aigu map)

Belle Gueule 6c Mont Pivot (Trois Pignons centre)

Prouesse 7b Near 95.2 (Trois Pignons north)

La Fissure des Alpinistes 5 Apremont (Apremont map)

Tempête 7c Traverse near Barbizon (Apremont map)

Attention Chef d'Oeuvre 7a Buthiers

The Prow 5+ Rocher d'Hércule (Mont Ussy)

Coeur de Lion 7a (Eléphant West)

Happy hunting!

LOOK NO HANDS

And while we're in the mood for lists, thanks to Marc le Menestrel for this selection of humbling fun and games for those who have done everything or who simply want to improve their footwork. All of these problems (some of which would be difficult with several hands!) can be done one or no-handed. Occasional use of elbows, shoulders or knees is at your discretion but some have been done without.

Bas Cuvier
  1B Le Sans les Mains (plan 1)
  12B La Dalle du Reveil-matin (plan 1)
  44B La Nationale one-handed (plan 2)
  2BI La Pogne (plan 1)
  6W La Défroquée one-handed (insert 1)
  12W La Chicorée one-handed (insert 2)

Apremont
  34R La Science Friction (plan 5)

Isatis
  13W (plan 1)
  La Zip Zut (plan 1)
  53W La Patinoire (plan 4) After initial pull over roof, feet and nothing else!

91.1
  9 and 9bR (plan 1)

Rocher Fin
  8B

This is just a tiny (and difficult) selection. In fact any off-vertical climb but particularly yellows and oranges can provide a challenge and a quick reminder of how hopeless your footwork is!

JUMPING AROUND

Here's a small selection of very hard dynos – the hardest in the forest?

St Germain	Cuisiniere
Megalight	Hale Bopp
Isatis	**La Canche**
Le Vin Aigre	Jacadi
95.2	
Ange Naïf	

There's no word for boulderer in French unless you're a Fontainebleau local and preferably skilled in the strange art of climbing here, in which case you are a **Bleausard** and you know all the following vocabulary...

un bloc	boulder
le bloc	bouldering
faire du bloc	to boulder
un mur	wall
une dalle	slab
une fissure	crack
un dièdre	corner/groove
un arête/angle	arete
un toit	roof
surplomb	overhang
un dévers	overhanging wall
raide	steep
déversant	overhanging
incliné	less than vertical
arrondi(e)	rounded
main gauche/droite	
	left/right hand
pied gauche/droit	
	left/right foot
une (bonne/mauvaise) prise	
	a (good/ bad) hold
un bacquet	jug
un trou	hole/pocket
mono(doigt)	one-finger pocket
bidoigt	two-finger pocket
un gratton	small edge/crimp
une réglette	edge
une verticale	sidepull
une inversée	undercut
un aplat	sloper
une bossete	boss
une pince	pinch
une prise taillée	chipped hold
magnésie	chalk
pof/résine	resin
paillasson/tapis	mat

strapal	finger tape
un mouvement	move
un pas	move
un réta(blissement)	mantelshelf
la sortie	the exit/finish
le départ	the start
un pied-main	high step up with foot next to hand
basculier	to rock-over
une lolotte	egyptian
jambe en drapeau	flag a leg
crochet de talon	heel hook
crochet de pointe	toe hook
dulfer	layback
porte de grange	barndoor
un yaniro	figure of 4
bloquer	to lock off
bloquage	a lock-off
bourriner	to crank
bourrin	adj. for above
coincer	to jam
arquer	to crimp
en arqué	crimped
en tendu	open-handed
en oppo(sition)	pulling with hand, pushing with foot normally vertical holds and Lhand Lfoot or RR
en épaule	locked off next to your shoulder - forearm horizontal
carre interne	instep
carre externe	outside of foot
en pointe	toe of shoe
croiser	to cross
un croisé	a crossing move
	And for crosses with extra long reaches...
un crawl	...crosses over and...
un derviche	...crosses under
statique	static
dynamique	er...obvious, no?
le ballant	the swing you have to control

when your feet cut loose.

tomber	to fall
une (mauvaise) chute	
	a (bad) fall
une talonade	hurting your heel in fall
sauter	to jump off
jeter	to jump/dyno
une parade	a spot
parer	to spot
pareur	spotter

"Pouvez-vous me parer?"

"Can you spot me?"

(très) beau bloc, superbe, etc

a very good problem

une bouse	a very poor problem
	(a cow pat)
éxpo(sé)	bold/a problem with a bad
	landing
délicat	delicate
physique	strenuous
à doigt	fingery
technique	technical
athlétique	gymnastic
aléatoire	precarious
morpho	height dependent/reachy
technique de pied	footwork
facile	easy
difficile	difficult
dur	hard
sec	dry
gras/glaque	greasy
mouille	wet

"(C'est) biscuit!" what you'll be told if you
use an 'illegal' hold.

"Il l'a randonné." "He walked it."

"Il n'y a que dalle!" "There's knack all!"
(handy for hard slabs or sand
bags where no one warned you
about the horrific exit mantel.)

un steak a flapper

'Je me suis fait un steak."

"I've ripped a flapper."

"Je me suis fait mal"

"I('ve) hurt myself"

"J'ai les bouteilles"

"I'm pumped"

"Je suis daubé" "I'm knackered"

"allez!" general expression of
encouragement

muler comme une âne "to mule like a donkey"
Strong folk with poor footwork
or no technique are often
tempted to do this.

un boeuf	thug
boeuf	thuggish

Finally, you rarely hear people say "I can't do
it," at Bleau. Rather, they say "Je ne le com-
prends pas" - "I don't understand it"....